To our parents,

Maggie & Clarence Geissinger

Esther & Erwin Schantz

For their love and continual support;
For their faith and encouragement;
For their example of living Godly lives;
For their showing us the importance
of living honest and trustworthy lives.

It is the greatest gift to share a Christian
heritage that goes back many generations.
Although they each have gone to their eternal rewards,
we are thankful to have been able to enjoy
Dan's mother through her 100th birthday.

Hand in Hand by Faith, by Dan and Mildred Schantz.
Forwarded by Alma J. Geosits.

Scripture quotations are taken from the Holy Bible, New American Standard
Version (NASV), 1995.

Photos. We are grateful for the hundreds of pictures, advertisements and
documents that were made available to Dan and Mildred from family, friends and
employees.

Interviews. Over forty interviews were conducted with the friends, family and
employees. Some contributions are found as quoted; others as contributions to a
time or an event. All those interviewed, whether face-to-face, by phone or email
graciously shared their stories and their admiration of Dan and Mildred. This
biography would not have been complete without their input.

Published by: Printworks & Company Inc.
Cover Design by: Printworks & Company Inc.

Printed in United States
ISBN Information

ISBN 978-0-692-49931-3
90000>

Hand in Hand by Faith

Part 1

Part 2

Part 3

Part One

"Tell it to your children, and let your children tell it to their children and their children to the next generation."
Joel 1:3

To tell of the legacy of a couple is to share the stories of their life moments, their memories, their vision for a future together and their promises to God and each other. The shared knowledge of their life's journey has no beginning day and it is the hope of the story that it will not have an ending date. Sown are the seeds of their faith, their passions, and their work into the fertile ground of the next generation. In time, the harvest will yield a bounteous portion of guidance needed by us all to live full lives.

Dan and Mildred Schantz lives have touched generations through their friendships, their businesses and their charity. Many regard them as their surrogate parents and their guidance as life changing. Their business and their travel have taken them miles and continents away from their Quakertown home. Their family, friends and employees retell and elaborate on the stories with love and laughter and some tears. The stories are filled with affirmation of Dan and Mildred's work ethic, benevolence, commitment and above all faith.

The company mission statement rings true each day of business for the past and present employees of Dan Schantz Farm. They are honored to be a part of this endeavor. They work hard until the job is done. There is satisfaction with each day's work; from the hint of new seedling growth in a vast spread of a greenhouse prepared for the approaching new season to the satisfaction of an end-of-season freshly swept empty greenhouse floor ready for the next plantings. The statement truly reflects the partnership and vision of Dan and Mildred. Simply stated; thoughtful; forward thinking.

The mission of Dan Schantz Farm is to produce the world's finest flowers and fall ornamentals. We are committed to providing the most up-to-date varieties of the highest quality to all our customers; providing prompt, courteous service, accurate and complete information, and integrity in all our dealings.

We are committed to participating in and improving the quality of life in the community in which we live. We believe in the fundamental value of long-term relationships with our customers and our employees. Dan Schantz Farm is dedicated to providing a safe and Christian environment for all employees with morality and honesty as the framework for all present and future plans.

 Dan Schantz Farm *& Greenhouses, LLC*

The LOGO of the Dan Schantz Farm and Greenhouses, LLC has its own story. Ideas for a LOGO came from their gifted art and advertising employees. Dan did not believe any of those submitted for his approval were the right look. Indisputably, Dan knows when he sees what he likes and when he sees what he does not like. Mildred sketched out a suggested design; a flower with a jack o' lantern pumpkin at the center. The design without the jack o' lantern face met with Dan's approval. The final product is a collaborative effort from the couple whose vision, faith and hard work are the story behind the product.

Mildred's Story

T he fourth child born to Clarence and Maggie Geissinger on May 29, 1932 was their daughter, Mildred. She joined her three siblings during what must have been the busy planting season for her family of Pennsylvania Dutch farmers. Her two older sisters, Ada (7 years older) and Ruth (3.5 years older), and older brother Isaac (9 years older) would be delighted to welcome a new baby into their home. "The Baby" would become the long-standing and endearing nickname for their little sister, Mildred. Her happy childhood began and she grew within a community of neighbors and extended family who worshipped and farmed together through the seasons and the years.

Mildred's hardworking parents were sharecropping farmers on a small dairy cattle operation owned by her father's Uncle, Harvey Landis. The field work was done with horses and their small herd was milked by hand. She doesn't recall Mom and Pop ever complaining, raising their voices or arguing; except the time that Pop went to auction to buy horses and chose to come home with two mules instead! The family's main source of income was from the "milk check;" money they earned from the sale of milk delivered in milk cans to Landis Dairy in Quakertown borough.

This was a time when our country faced the economic crisis of the Great Depression. Despite some of the worst times in the country's history, the family faithfully worked hard to stay on the land and to make a living. During this era, farmers continued to be innovative and some of the most revolutionary US agricultural technologies came along: bigger and better tractors with new rubber wheels, combines that ended the era of threshing, hybrid seed corn, the first modern pesticides and electricity and indoor plumbing.

Mildred fondly recalls their busy life on the farm. She always enjoyed the hard work and didn't question it. She preferred chores that would keep her outdoors over any that would assist Mom in the house. Her chores as a youngster included hand pumping well water for the cows and taking care of the chickens. It was all part of the life she knew, "whatever had to be done, we did it and were happy with it." The Geissinger children never had much, but they never knew they were poor. They always had everything they needed.

Mildred began her formal education at Brick Tavern School, a one-room school in Milford Township. She walked about a mile from the farm to school with her sister, Ruth. At Brick Tavern school, about twenty-five children in grades one through eight were taught by the same teacher. The teacher had the responsibility each day to arrive early and build a fire in the black pot belly stove, teach all subjects to all grades, do playground duty and clean the building. There was no running water or well so the students took turns going to a neighbor for a pail of water for drinking.

School days and farm chores filled Mildred's busy days. There was time to enjoy life, too. This young tomboy relished leisure time outside with her friends and her older brother, Isaac. In winter there was sledding on shovels and ice skating on

Mildred (right) and her sister, Ruth enjoy shove sleds, 1940

the ponds; on warm summer days there was playing ball with a broken shovel handle bat and other games they made up. The athletic Mildred could keep up with and do better than most of the boys! Her neighbor, Dan Schantz, counted on her to be his catcher. Often on a Sunday there was time for visiting with nearby family and friends from the community. Her mother kept the kitchen pantry well stocked and ready for a quick meal. There was always room at the table for company.

Mildred was about ten years old when there was talk at home of World War II. Her parents read the reports in the local papers and shared with their children what they needed to know. They bought meat and sugar as well a gasoline with their allotted ration coupons. They heard a lot about milk, eggs and meat being purchased through the "black market". Her parents were most concerned that her brother, Isaac, would be drafted. He was able to

1942 Union School
Left photo: Mildred in Grade 5 (2nd row, first on right);
Right photo: Dan in Grade 3 (2nd row, right)

receive a draft deferment for farmers, a common practice at this time in rural farm areas due to the severe shortage of farm laborers.

In spite of early WWII inflated farmland prices, Pop purchased a farm along Old Bethlehem Pike in Zion Hill in the spring of 1942. He borrowed money from Henry Longacre to purchase the farm. Young Mildred felt they were doing okay to move to a farm with electricity instead of kerosene lanterns and a gas light in the kitchen. Indoor plumbing would come later. The Geissinger family walked their cows and farm equipment about two miles north on Old Bethlehem Pike on the early spring day they moved to the new farm. Moving just a few miles north meant a transfer to Union School, a one-room school located on the corner of Grant Road and Old Bethlehem Pike. It was here that Mildred attended grades five through eight. Mildred's teacher that first year at Union school was Esther Schantz, Dan's mother. Following WWI and the Depression, the Milford Township school board laid off many of its married female teachers, including Esther Schantz, in order to make more jobs available to men. During WWII, men were called to serve in the Armed Forces and the school board begged women to return to their positions. In 1942 Mrs. Schantz was called back to teach. She reluctantly returned and taught for one year. Dan was in third grade and Mildred was in fifth grade that school year.

The Geissinger Farm operation quickly grew on this larger property, a tractor was purchased, their milking herd was increased and chickens became a mainstay. Their milk would be picked up at the farm by

Lehigh Valley Dairy, Allentown. Her family would also begin growing tomatoes under contract for Campbell's Soup Company in Camden, New Jersey. Mildred, "the Tomato Picking Boss" was in charge of overseeing the neighborhood kids hired to help pick acres of tomatoes. Twelve to fifteen youngsters, including her neighbor, Dan Schantz, were paid eight to ten cents per basket picked. They delighted in doing it. There were many battles with the rotten ones. The filled baskets were skillfully loaded on trucks and driven to Camden, New Jersey. On those busy, long days they would go to bed tired and happy. The Geissinger family like many other farming families in the Quakertown and Lehigh Valley, would continue to grow tomatoes for Campbell's Soup until the mid-seventies.

A trolley ride to town from just outside her back door and a seven block walk was Mildred's transportation arrangement to attend Quakertown High School. Public school buses became available in her junior year and after she got her license at 16, she occasionally drove her Pop's car. At Quakertown High School she could buy her lunch for 26 cents and enjoy a good Pennsylvania Dutch style cooked meal in the cafeteria. Mildred took business as her High School course of study. She began music lessons in High School and learned to play the guitar. Though she would not ever play in public, she felt she had played well enough and purchased her own electric guitar. Mildred most of all enjoyed participating in the sports programs offered in Physical Education class; softball was her favorite. She also enjoyed field hockey and basketball. She was a very good athlete and was encouraged to play on Quakertown's High School varsity teams. She did not participate because of her responsibilities at the family farm. Mildred graduated in 1950. After a summer of working on the family farm, she took a job as the first secretary/ bookkeeper the Longacre Poultry Farms business would employ. She earned $1.25 per hour, a good rate at that time.

PERIOD ENDING	TOTAL HOURS	EARNINGS				DEDUCTIONS								NET PAY	NO.
		REGULAR	OVERTIME	OTHER	TOTAL	FEDERAL INC. TAX	F.I.C.A.	A	B	C	D	E	TOTAL		
11-7-53	40¾	50 00	141		51 41	7 70	77						8 47	42 94	1436

A paystub from one of Mildred's pay checks, November 1953

8

While working a full-time job, Mildred shared with her family the responsibilities of the busy Geissinger farm operation. She also was the first secretary at Swamp Mennonite Church, preparing the weekly bulletin in a print ready format in time for it to be produced by the Mennonite Bookstore in Souderton.

The Geissinger family is deeply rooted in Mennonite heritage. Pop Geissinger and his family attended Swamp Mennonite Church (SMC) on Rosedale Road. They faithfully served the church as the caretakers. Generations of the Geissinger family have worshipped at Swamp. It was Philip Geissinger who in 1847 donated the land on which the first meetinghouse was built. It remains today as the education wing of the current SMC structure. In the 30's and 40's the congregation met every other week for worship and held Sunday School on the off weeks—these were often the weeks the Geissinger family enjoyed visiting or having company at their home.

At fourteen, Mildred accepted Jesus as her personal Savior. Her life verse is Ephesians 2:8, *"For by grace you have been saved through faith, and that not of yourselves; it is a gift from God."* (ASV) She was baptized and became a member of SMC that same year. Through High School Mildred was active in the youth gatherings and fund raising projects. Sharing in the strong Mennonite tradition of service, Mildred spent eight weeks in Minnesota teaching Bible School during the summer of 1951.

Dan's Story

T he first child born to Erwin M. and Esther Mae (Longacre) Schantz on March 29, 1934 was a son, Daniel W. Schantz. Three years later his sister, Mary Alice was born. Their happy childhood was lived out in the same farmhouse

Dan in the chicken coup at his family hatchery.

just off Rosedale Road in Quakertown where their mother was born and raised. Purchased from Dan's grandfather, Henry R. Longacre, the 23 acre fifth generation family property was the center of the family poultry business operation. The hatchery, for primarily baby chicks and baby turkeys had a 100,000 egg capacity, was considered a large operation at that time. Hatched chicks were packed and shipped from their farm to markets over much of the Mid-Atlantic region and as far as Puerto Rico. Poultry was dressed on the farm on Thursday and sold with eggs, a variety of home-grown produce and his mother's home-made salads and baked goods at markets in Philadelphia and Allentown each weekend.

From a very young age, Dan and his sister, Mary Alice were busy helpers on the farm and at the markets. On market days they would waken at 3 AM to go along with their parents to their retail stands. Dan assisted with customers and made change when he was four years old. This would be the beginning of a keen interest in retail markets as well as hands on business experiences. Working alongside his parents, a young eager Dan was learning the buying and negotiating knowledge of the busy meat and produce markets.

Dan's education began at home at his mother side. Esther Schantz was a teacher prior to her marriage. She would often read to her children. Basic math skills were practiced and mastered very young by Dan and his sister under their parents' guidance at the markets. His school days in grades one through grade six were held at nearby Union School, a one room schoolhouse for 25 to 30 area children. While in third grade he was taught by his mother for one year. Though encouraged by the

Milford Township School Board, his mother felt she could not continue to teach as she was too hard on her own children. Dan was characterized by his Union school teacher as a "quick thinker" and was promoted to grade eight after completing grade six. He completed grade eight at Steinsburg School. These were happy times for Dan. He is sure that skipping seventh grade was so he could "catch up" to his neighbor, Mildred Geissinger. He already had a growing fondness for this friend and schoolmate.

Dan would soon also develop a passion for growing things. The Schantz farm property was a natural setting for a young boy to acquire a farming spirit. When springtime came it was time to think of planting. Dan would become and is still known as the "produce farmer." "What a gratifying experience to plant seeds and watch them grow into plants and produce all those garden goodies," Dan recalled to an audience on the occasion of his receiving the Mid-Atlantic Master Farmer Award in 1987.

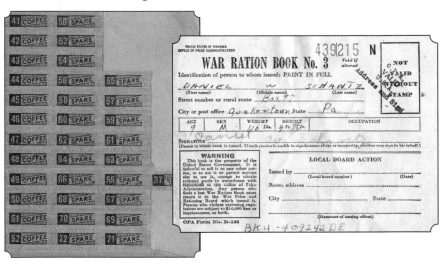

During the time of World War II, Dan would travel to Reading Terminal Market in Philadelphia with his father. Even with the war on, the vendors managed to provide a surprising variety of provisions. Despite labor shortages and other problems brought on by the war, 97 percent of the stalls at the market were occupied in 1944. World War II was a time when the rationing of food also brought about a scarcity rationed meat. Young Dan and his father were aware of farmer's selling black market chicken and meat at the Market, but Dan's father would not ever participate in such activity. Careful planning by his father and mother, and their own farm crop of produce and poultry kept the Schantz family supplied with what was needed during this depressed economic era.

When he was ten years old, Dan joined the local 4H and would win numerous awards for his capons and showmanship of steer. Before he turned thirteen, Dan was earning his first retail income by cutting and cleaning dandelion greens at the farm and then selling them at a table across the aisle from his Mother's poultry stand in Allentown.

Trapping muskrats was a source of good income for a young man on the farm in the forties. One year Dan caught over 300 of them; 34 the first night. He chuckles and recalls that he was after two muskrats in burrows just off the bank at his parent's Rosedale Road farm. Their burrowed holes were just four feet apart. The holes were occupied by two skunks, not muskrats. He got sprayed on that day of trapping. And he also got sent home from school because he smelled like a skunk! He gave his mom $50 dollars from his trapping earnings so she could purchase a much needed coat. She had been waiting and saving to purchase one. With Dan's gift, she bought two.

Dan was well known as a strong, hard-working young man. His maturing negotiating skills and business savvy were mixed with youthful risk taking. While offloading 134 pound bags of feed with a hired worker at his father's farm he offered a dare. He boasted that he could carry the bag out the lane down to the creek and back. They bet a week's wages. Dan put his broad shoulders into the challenge and carried the bag down the 1200 feet (four football field lengths) of the lane. Dan won the bet. He didn't settle for a week's wages, instead he took the offer of tickets to see the Phillies play ball at Connie Mac Stadium.

Dan attended Quakertown High School where he took the Vocational Agricultural course. He belonged to the Future Farmers of America and 4H. Though athletic and encouraged to play football and varsity sports, Dan chose to continue to be passionately involved in retail and farming projects. He rented his first farm land when he was sixteen years old. The twenty acre tract of land belonged to his grandfather, Alan Schantz. He soon added additional rented acreage from the Links family in Steinsburg. He would rent this tract of land for fifty-six years. By the time he was a

High School senior, he had 80 to 100 acres of rented land, on which he grew corn, grains, and soy beans. His farming projects included raising beef cattle, furrowing sows, raising capons, turkeys and suckling pigs. His extensive farming and retail projects required working long hours after school and on Saturdays. Dan's first planting of sweet corn was during a very hot and dry period. The ears of corn were small and not very good. On an unusually hot day Dan picked and bagged the crop by himself. Dan loaded the bagged crop on a borrowed truck and took it to Philadelphia Dock Street Market to sell. He sold none of it. He lost the crop and he declares he lost fifteen pounds off his weight that day.

When he had saved enough money to buy either a car or a tractor sixteen year old Dan chose to spend $2,500 on a new Oliver 66 Row Crop Tractor with plow and cultivator. After years of use, the tractor has been restored and is kept on display in an enclosed pagoda at the Schantz family home.

Dan beside the restored Oliver 66 tractor outside their family home.

It remains a fond reminder to him and Mildred of their youth.

Dan helped out his Dad whenever he could or was needed. He supplied the beef for his father's Allentown grocery store each week. If he did not have a steer ready, he would purchase one or two at auction. During holiday times of peak sales at his Dad's store and the early morning market at the Allentown Fairgrounds, turkeys were often purchased from growers in the Shenandoah Valley of Virginia. They had to be trucked to the farm in time to be dressed for Thanksgiving and Christmas sales.

When he was 16 or 17, Dan and a hired man drove a truck full of empty crates to a turkey farm in Sunbury, PA to pick up a load of turkeys. Dan was driving, fell asleep and rolled the truck. The truck landed on its wheels. They continued on their trip with no problems or additional stops. Dan still loves to drive. And he is known for his fast driving. Safe, but fast. There would be many tales of his driving, though an early one was a local adventure with his cousins. As teenagers filled with daring they were known to have driven cars on the trolley tracks. They would get the car on the track width at Brick Tavern and ride to Main Street in Quakertown. The debate continues as to whether or not the trolleys were still running at that time.

At sixteen, Dan grew two acres of tomatoes for the Campbell Soup Company in Camden New Jersey. There were many local farmers under contract and doing well selling their tomatoes to the Campbell Company. Dan saw the opportunity and returns for investment. Much of the harvest season during September he would pick crop during the day and would often make late night deliveries with his Dad's truck to the Campbell's Camden, New Jersey plant. His senior year he would miss seventy-two sessions (half days) of classes in High School. Dan would receive the Keystone Farmer's Award in his senior year of High school prior to his graduation in 1951.

Dan's mother had carefully saved money from the earnings of the produce grown on the farm and her baked goods sold at market to provide for the college education of her two children. Dan would choose not to take the time to go to college but would use his share to further his farming and produce business. More than material help, Dan was blessed by his parent's abundant encouragement and strong faith.

Dan always knew that Sunday was the day to go to church. His father's family had strong ties to the Lutheran faith and his mother to her Mennonite heritage and faith. Mother was a member at Swamp Mennonite Church (SMC) and Father at St John's Lutheran, Spinnerstown. Dan and his family would attend each church every other Sunday. At 14, Daniel accepted Jesus as his personal Savior. Romans 1:16a, *"For I am not ashamed of the gospel of Christ, for it is the power of God to salvation for everyone who believes."* (NASV) He attended catechism classes at both churches, but he chose to become a member at SMC. On the Sunday of his baptism Dan recalls that, "My father felt bad because I didn't choose to join the Lutheran church. He tied my tie for me the Sunday I joined Swamp. I couldn't tie my tie and he had tears in his eyes. He didn't say much, but he never really said much." Dan was an active leader in Mennonite Youth Fellowship. As president of the group, they arranged for an acre of land to grow tomatoes. The group worked the land, grew, harvested and sold the tomatoes at a stand at the Quakertown Farmer's Market and raised $3400. The funds were all sent to the mission work of Minnesota Northern Lights in Minnesota. This was the same organization where Mildred and others had done youth summer service. The group, under Dan's leadership, were service-minded, worked hard, had fun working together and set an example for future generations to raise funds and give back to the community and to mission outreach.

Courtship & Marriage

Sitting across the office desk from Dan, Mildred and he are able to communicate without words. Their's is a private story they quietly impart. It is one of love and mutual respect. It reflects the years they have shared and their commitment to kindness and forgiveness. They have learned to give and forgive and "get over it;" to compromise on what was best and not seek to get their own way.

How did they meet? That is hard to say. Was Mildred by her mother's side as a toddler when Dan's mother with her newborn son entered the woman's side of Swamp Mennonite Church? Their mothers no doubt shared stories of raising the children they loved and nurtured. They grew up in the same Sunday School class, ran in the church yard and made up games to play. If Dan was practicing his pitching, Mildred was the catcher. They went to school together and when Mildred could drive, Dan rode with her to High School. They dated each other and others over those High School years and would become more serious about each other in Dan's senior year of high school. Dates were often on Sunday evenings. They would attend area churches for services and hymn sings. The hymns were often sung acapella, a beautiful blending of voices in four-part harmony without instruments. Their favorites are well-known gospel hymns; *"Victory in Jesus"*, *"Wonderful Grace of Jesus"*, *"A Wonderful Savior is Jesus My Lord"*, and *"For God So Loved Us"* each song expresses their love of music in worship and praising God in song.

The first night that Dan went to her home to "call on" Mildred he recalls that his dad's Buick wouldn't start when he was ready to go home. He walked home that evening. There wasn't anything wrong with the car. Dan was nervous. He had sights set on a goal; Mildred, the girl up the road. By the time he was nineteen he had won her heart and affection. They announced their engagement at a gathering of their church young adults at Mildred's home. The cat was out of the bag. Mildred received a silver place setting service for twelve from Dan as an engagement gift. She still uses the set for holidays and special occasions.

On August 30, 1953, Dan and Mildred were married at Swamp Mennonite Church. The ceremony was held on a beautiful, sunny Sunday afternoon. Holding it on Sunday meant that many of their friends and family who went to markets on Saturday would be able to join them. Following a simple reception held at Coopersburg Fire Hall, the newlyweds honeymooned at Niagara Falls and through the Finger Lakes region of New York State in their first car, a 1950 Ford that Dan had bought that week.

On their return to Quakertown there was work to do. They were immediately busy picking acres of tomatoes for the Campbell's contract. Mildred is still not sure why they chose August to get married.

The newlyweds established their first home in Quakertown in a third floor rental in a converted barn along Old Bethlehem Pike at Koons Road. The rent was $55.00 a month. Conveniently, their apartment was also located just a short distance from both of their parent's farms. With the $2,000 Mildred had saved from her job at Longacre Poultry they purchased the furniture and carpets for their living room, bedroom and kitchen; and a refrigerator, too. Mildred still had her electric guitar when they got married. Dan traded it for a pig. This apartment would be their home for three and a half years.

Their newlywed days were filled with farming and markets, church activities and time with extended family and friends. Four young married couples from Swamp Mennonite would share the lasting bond of friendship. They served in leadership at Swamp Mennonite Church together, raised families and supported each other. The group would soon grow to six couples. Sometime in the late fifties they began to celebrate that friendship with an annual clambake each August. Fifty-five years later the remaining couples and spouses, children, grandchildren and great-grandchildren continue to gather for an annual clambake and to celebrate friendship and family.

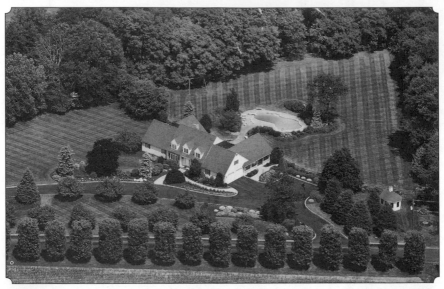

The Schantz home in Quakertown, PA.
Aerial View; Their home for the last 24 years; Pagoda building housing Dan's First tractor.

Their Children

As busy and full as their life together as married couple and business partners was Dan and Mildred desired to have children. Their lives would be filled with the joy a long-awaited child brings in the summer of 1961. Born on June 18, 1961, at just two-and-a half days old, Dan and Mildred received for adoption a son they named Thomas Lee Schantz. Mildred treasures the memories of this special time and recalls that he was a 'good baby and slept well' for them. Tommy was an active toddler who ran before he walked. He never slowed down, Dan remembers with a pleased smile. At just 9 months his first steps would find him just the right height to run under the kitchen table. And run he did. That was Tommy! Tommy went everywhere with Dan and Mildred on the farm property; outside to check on the field of a crop or in the sheds and greenhouses. Tommy enjoyed his busy days. He knew everyone. He loved being with everyone, and he loved being on the farm. One of young Tommy's favorite spots to visit was with the hired crews at their labor camp just up the road from the family farm house. He would often be found here at dinner time. One evening the youngster was not to be found. Everyone was charged with looking for him. He was found safe and sound asleep on a cot in the camp house. The farm was his playground and everyone his childhood friend.

Mildred had Tommy along with her in the station wagon one summer afternoon. The station wagon was the first new car she owned. She went to check on the crop of peas in a field off of Grant Road. She got out of the car to get a closer look some plants just a few feet away. Still in the car, young Tommy managed to put the car in gear. It rolled down a twenty-five foot embankment toward the wooded edge of the field. The car landed between two trees. Tommy was not hurt. God would continue to watch over their outgoing, active son.

On July 31, 1963 Dan and Mildred were blessed by receiving for adoption a daughter. Born on July 26, 1963, Connie Lynn was a joyful addition to their family. Mildred was content that they now had the ideal American family, two children; one boy and one girl. Blue eyed, curly blonde haired, beautiful Connie was an early talker. She could hold a conversation at just eighteen months.

Tommy and Connie in the chicken house at the Spinnerstown Farm, 1966. Connie's red bandana shirt was made for her by Ada, Mildred's sister.

Her vivacious personality won the hearts of those at the farm, greenhouses and markets. She was always friendly. She was an active, mischievous and adventurous little girl who loved to swim. As soon as she could find someone to be with they would be swimming; morning, afternoon and night. Dan and Mildred called her "our little fish."

Mildred and Tommy (center of photo) Allentown Fairgrounds Market.

As children, Tom and Connie went along and helped out at the markets. Dan Schantz Farm was now a family business. Tommy recalls making change and playing checkers during those early years. He loved just hanging out with his dad all day. It was a treat to go along with him on produce auction run. He would sleep in the truck during the very early morning drive to the produce market. Then watch his Dad in action buying melons, closing the deals and loading the truck. At their Allentown Farmer's Market stand young Connie took naps on the stacks of bags under the counter. Connie with fondness recalls doing her part at the family produce stand at the Farmer's Market. She and Tom stood on apple crates and called out to the Market customers the prices for produce. "Grapes. Three pounds a dollar!" They learned to weigh and bag produce and make change for customers. Dan would sit them down in the evenings with quarters, dimes, nickels and pennies. Teaching his young children as he had been taught by his parents to identify the coins and make combinations equal to a dollar and equal to the correct change for a dollar. He was patient with them as they practiced over and over and gave approval to their young efforts.

Gourds and pumpkins are a mainstay of the fall crop at Dan Schantz Farm even today. Connie would watch her mother expertly choose some of the perfect shape, color and size from the farm field; the best of each type of gourd. As a small child she would have been delighted to have some of their best crop to decorate her house. Instead, Mildred's select gourds would be carefully and skillfully dried and the seeds preserved for the next season's crop. Life on the farm for the Schantz children was a story of the fruit of each season and the preparation for the next season.

The years pass quickly on a busy growing produce farm and Connie knew that it was becoming a bigger operation. She was too little to be out there but knew it was happening from her view of the expansion of greenhouses and the activity outside of the kitchen door. Her Dad was not around as much and her Mom was busier in the packing house and at the greenhouses. When they were old enough they helped out during summer and after school. But Connie and Tommy never knew it was work; it was fun and it was what you did.

There were two constants with the Schantz family. Family dinner was always together and Sunday was the time to go to church. After church there was dinner together and leisure afternoons of games and activities with extended family They enjoyed their children and made it a priority to do things together as a family. It was the life they knew; a balance of hard work and the best of fun that a rural farm and home could provide.

Like their Dad and Mom, Tommy and Connie were athletic children who enjoyed participating in sports. Tommy was involved and

Football photo of Tommy with Dan and Mildred at Bluffton College, Bluffton, Ohio

excelled in community little league, basketball and began playing midget football at age eight. Dan took off on a Saturday, his first in years to watch Tommy play in his first game. Tommy's main interest would stay with football. In High School he played both offensive and defensive positions for Southern Lehigh. At Bluffton College he played wide end receiver. Dan and Mildred made every effort to be at their children's games. They drove out Friday afternoon, stayed over en route and were in Bluffton, Ohio on Saturday morning for home games. Mildred recalls feeling his pain every time he was tackled as he reached up for the ball. She still doesn't know how he managed to hold onto them. Tommy remembers his mom would bring a care package for him that always had pretzels and Good & Plenty candy. Connie participated in softball, track and field events of discus and shot put and played field hockey in High School. She also found time to be active in drama in High School. At Eastern Mennonite University in Harrisonburg, Virginia she played Field Hockey. And Dan and Mildred traveled to be on the sidelines for her home games.

The first summertime extended vacation with Connie and Tommy was a three week family trip to California. They flew to San Francisco, California, rented a car and drove and did sightseeing all along the California coast and on to Salt Lake City, Utah. The family then drove all the way home. Tommy and Connie were 14 and 12 at the time and eager to get home; Connie to her friends and the pool at their home and Tommy to his baseball team. The trip was a great time together as family. Many family trips were also taken to Disney World. The first time was soon after the Florida park opened. This trip was often taken on President's Day weekend so little or no school was missed. The Schantz family also had the opportunity to go to the Jersey shore for a week or two in the summer. Often Tommy and Connie would invite friends to go along to the rented beach house in Ocean City, NJ. Dan would spend time to do produce buying during these vacations. He traveled to the Philadelphia Food Center and also the Vineland, NJ produce auction for items they did not grow but would do well in their markets. Winter family trips were taken to Old Forge, NY. Their three snowmobiles provided carefree days on the miles of snowmobile trails. More extensive trips were made to Hawaii (where they found that they Hawaiians couldn't keep their hands off of Connie's blond curls), Puerto Rico, and to several bowl games; the

Sugar Bowl, the Orange Bowl and the Rose Bowl parade and game. And wherever they traveled Dan would stop at roadside stands, markets and fields to inspect the produce and compare the growing conditions and techniques. They drove out to tour a pineapple plantation field on the Hawaii trip. Dan stopped as to take a closer look

The view from their seats at the Rose Bowl Parade

at the plants. They were quickly greeted by the owner who must have felt they had gotten a bit too close. Later this same owner gave Dan several ripe pineapples. The kitchen staff at their hotel cut them up for the group's breakfast the next morning. Tommy and Connie soon knew that wherever they went they would meet someone who knew Dan. His reputation and his business connections were respected and well-known. They also knew that trips were planned so as much as was possible they would be back in time for church on Sunday morning. It was and remains a priority for Dan and Mildred.

Tommy and Connie are proud of their Dad and Mom. They both have fond memories of traveling with their Dad to the Philadelphia Wholesale Produce Market. Dad was "famous" there. Everyone knew him and greeted him. Dan would return the greeting with a "Whatcha got for me?" They watched as deals were sealed with a handshake. And Dan would quickly move onto the next vendor. Nothing was written. Dan kept mental notes of how much he was spending, how many pounds of produce he purchased and the square footage that produce would fill in each truck. His ability to recall numbers and mentally calculate totals is a rare gift. One which his children are quick to affirm and brag on! If they were at auction he was selling from the truck and keeping close eye on the money box and the making of change. He could estimate with near accuracy the end of day's total before it was counted.

Family photo. This picture was used in an early summer advertising booklet.

Her children will tell you that their mom, Mildred, is a gifted grower and mentor with an artistic eye for display and advertising. Through her knowledge of the seasons, soil, seeds, plants and the growing conditions she guided and taught the greenhouse workers to grow the best possible produce and later plants and bedding flowers. She taught them by consistent example and her personal creeds; "first you get ready to work, then you work," "if it is worth doing, it is worth doing well," and "God gave you two hands, use them both." Mildred made sure work was both productive and fun.

Their children would be witness to a strong faith, a disciplined work ethic, a commitment to growing a business to provide for their family, a business that would employ many and a passion to share generously with those in need. Dan and Mildred taught their children that all they had God had given them. Their Dad never seemed to be worried. He trusted in the deal. And the handshakes. Their Mom was unshakable. If things did not go well they knew that God would provide: "the will, the grace and the power to move on." They walk by faith. They trust and they show kindness. They walk humbly. They forgive and move forward. And they have stood by their children and grandchildren.

Dan muses that perhaps they were not strict enough as parents. They waited so long before they got them both. A rare reflective comment for Dan. He and Mildred are devoted to their children their grandchildren and great grandchildren. There is unconditional love and quiet concern for each of them.

Today Tommy is a partner in the ownership of the Steel Ice Center and the Sand's Event Center. Tommy married Ann in 1988. Tommy adopted Ann's sons Tad and Brandon. He and Ann live in Quakertown. They share in the busy lives of their three adult children and three grandchildren.

Ann shares her thoughts, with heartfelt love for Dan and Mildred:
Tad, Brandon and I had the pleasure of becoming part of the Schantz family in 1988. Marrying their son, my soulmate, Tom, in 1990. They welcomed us with open arms and have embraced us into their family from day one. Mom and Dad are truly the most loving and generous people I know. We have had the pleasure of spending many holidays and vacations with them. Mom is known for her wonderful cooking (especially dessert – as long as she doesn't put raisins in apple pies and makes candied sweet potatoes even when Niki isn't going to be there) . . . Some of my fondest memories include family bike rides to breakfast in Ocean City and wearing yellow Mickey Mouse ponchos while it rained in Disney World!

Connie serves as the Manager of the Cut Flower Department at the Dan Schantz Greenhouse and Cut Flower Outlet Lehigh Street retail store in Allentown. She and her two young adult children live in Coopersburg.

The Schantz Family 2014
Clockwise from upper left: Dan and Mildred and their family;
Connie and her children; Tommy with his wife, Ann and their family;
Tommy and Ann with their grandchildren.

The Gift of Family

Mildred ~ Brother, Isaac Geissinger;
Sisters, Ada Rosenberger, Ruth Longacre
Dan ~ Sister, Mary Alice Conrad
One Son, Tommy and his wife, Ann
One daughter, Connie
5 Grandchildren ~Niki and her husband, Josiah
Tad and his wife, Erin, Brandon and his wife, Lauren,
Andrew and Chelsie
3 Great grandchildren, Callen, Millie and Riley
26 Nieces and Nephews
73 Grand Nieces and Nephews

Grammy and Pop-pop
Family comes first.

Their five grandchildren and their three great grandchildren bring them joy. As a child, Niki, their first grandchild, spent most weekends and much of her summers with Dan and Mildred. She had her own room in their home. When their son Tom and Ann married, they were blessed with two grandsons, Tad and Brandon. And they were blessed again when Andrew and Chelsie, their daughter Connie's two children came along. They have traveled to attend school functions, concerts and sports events, awards ceremonies and graduations. Dan and Mildred "love them, spoil them and send them to their own homes."

Their home has always been open to their children and grandchildren. It has been a family gathering place and a retreat from the cares of the world. Dan and Mildred still gather as many of the family as they can for holidays, reunions and life events. The food is homemade and flavored with Mildred's exceptional cooking and baking and the fun and memories are endless. The gathering's priority is always that everyone was spending time together and everyone was enjoying themselves.

L to R: Andrew Schantz, Niki Scheick, Brandon Schantz, Chelsie King, Tad Schantz sitting in front of a well-remembered blue flocked Christmas tree.

Holidays are a special time to share with family. Christmas is remembered for trees sprayed with blue flock, Mildred's cut-out cookies, stockings filled with fun and useful goodies and games from the hallway closet. An annual monetary Christmas gift from Grammy and Pop-Pop is $100 presented to them in single ones. Chelsie remembers a year when she counted her pile of ones. Out loud. Slowly. Just old enough to be able to count to one hundred, each bill was counted and neatly stacked. Just to be sure. She need not have doubted.

Vacationing together was a big deal for each of them. Memories of summer days spent in Ocean City and winter trips to Florida and Disney World are fondly recalled. There was rainy day in Disney World when they all got yellow ponchos; Tom, Ann, their three children and Dan and Mildred. Almost every visitor in the park that day had on a yellow poncho. Dan and Mildred remember having a hard time keeping track of everyone! On a trip with daughter, Connie and her family, when Chelsie was but a toddler, Pop-Pop purchased a BBQ turkey drumstick to share. When young Chelsie had a taste she would not give it up. Mildred chuckles as she recalls how amazing it was to see Chelsie's little hand holding such a big treat. Tad, Brandon and Niki were promised that Pop-Pop would buy each one a toy or stuffed animal while they traveled together in Florida with their parents and Dan and Mildred. Their first stop was Sea World. Niki almost immediately spotted a black and white stuffed whale, Shamu. Pop-Pop told her that he would get it for her but maybe she would see something at Disney world she would rather have. Shamu was left behind. As it happened they would see a lot at Disney World. Tad and Brandon found their favorites, but Niki still had her heart set on a stuffed Shamu, at Sea World. Pop-Pop kept his word. On the way to the airport to return home they would stop by Sea World and get a Shamu. At Sea World the person at the service counter told Dan that he would need to pay for a pass for the day in order to enter the park. Dan explained that he just wanted to go in for a minute to buy a Shamu. He was finally admitted to the park, bought Niki a Shamu and they all got on the plane to go home. Happy. There were also many day trips. Niki remembers riding on the hump of the front seat with Dan at the wheel of his Lincoln Town Car. They felt special and loved every time they were with Dan and Mildred. Dan would put business aside and join them in the ocean, out for bike rides, on the boardwalk, playing miniature golf, in shops and at shows. Mildred notes that the grandchildren were not aware of the early morning phone calls to the farm office and with business contacts. Dan was never really far away from the business he built.

Each of their grandchildren has had firsthand employment experience at the farm that Dan and Mildred built together. They have gotten their hands dirty and their backs sore. They have smiled at customers and treated others with kindness and generosity. They know the hard work and commitment it has taken to build the business. And they have an appreciation for the people working at Dan Schantz Farm. They have learned the lessons of giving people opportunities when others doubted. They have seen their beloved grandfather "never really look at the past, believe in the fact that a second chance was needed, and always believe that the opportunity he was giving someone was the first step they needed to help turn their life in the right direction."

The grandchildren are quick to acknowledge their grandparent's support of their young adult decisions and their education. Schooling has been generously paid for and the emotional support each has needed in their own way has been given. Grammy and Pop-Pop know what to say. They know how to encourage hard work and support their dreams. The support is unconditional. They are always available and always just a phone call away. Their grandchildren love to hear Pop-Pop's sending words of "carry on," and their beloved Grammy's , "okeydokey." These familiar words offer them assurances of the years of love and support of their grandparents. Most importantly Grammy and Pop-Pop's lives tell their faith story. The seeds of faith have been planted. And it is valued by each of them. They know their home is centered on that faith. They know the business is based on that faith. They see that faith worked out through their grandparent's generosity, kindness to others and caring actions. They respect their lifelong attendance and support of Swamp Mennonite Church. When youngsters they have felt Pop-Pops pinch to settle in the pews and have been quieted by a Werther's candy from Grammy's purse. They hear the voice of their grandfather offering a familiar grace at a family meal. And they each have made their own way in living a life of faith. The Christian faith their grandparent's taught them.

Perhaps it is Brandon's reflection that best speaks for all the grandchildren:

> *When we (the grandchildren) were little, I always remember the story of how when Pop-Pop was about 16 years old, he made a decision that would kick start his career and pave the way for a life defined by the reciprocation of hard work and success. He could either; join the likes of many other licensed drivers and purchase a car, or he could purchase a tractor, which, unknowingly at the time, would be the start of a floral empire. That decision didn't mean much to me growing up. I thought it was cute and noble, but never thought about it the way I do now. I remember the day my father, Tom Schantz, had that tractor refurbished for him for Father's Day after it had been sitting, humbly oxidizing between greenhouses at the farm. The way Pop-Pop gazed, eyes filling, at that tractor was burned into my memory, but I still didn't quite know why.*

> *We all got older and went to our separate universities, focusing on our passions, plowing through our own fields, when I finally started to understand that heart-felt gaze. When Pop-Pop looked at that tractor, he didn't see a machine. He saw courage. He saw fear. He saw achievement. He saw Love. It was the courage to go where his heart pulled him, putting aside hardship and fear while maintaining a constant, vivid picture of his dreams.*

> *As a 27 year old musician, I have faced more professional rejection than most do in a life. But I continuously find myself looking at my instruments the same way Pop-Pop looked at his tractor. Without a word, he taught me to never stop trying to accomplish the things that bring me joy in this life. I have taken and taught thousands of lessons in my life, but that is one I will always keep with me.*

And Niki, now a mother of her own young daughter snuggles her child and remembers Grammy singing a simple lullaby to calm her; *"by o baby, by o baby by."* She knows love.

Thank you Grammy and Pop-Pop.

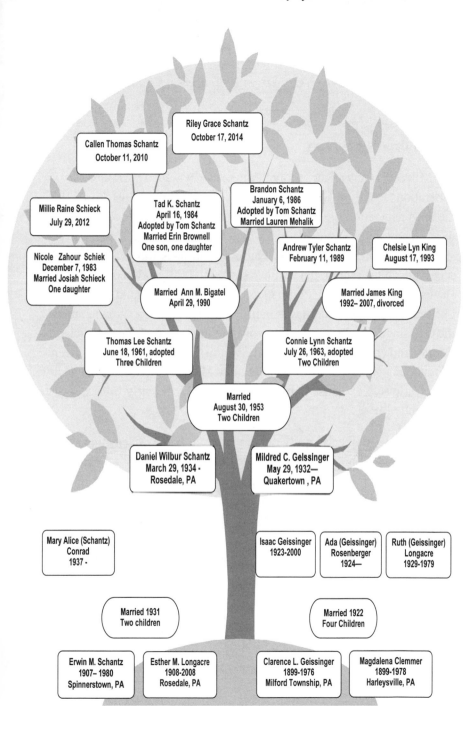

Riley Grace Schantz
October 17, 2014

Callen Thomas Schantz
October 11, 2010

Brandon Schantz
January 6, 1986
Adopted by Tom Schantz
Married Lauren Mehalik

Millie Raine Schieck
July 29, 2012

Tad K. Schantz
April 16, 1984
Adopted by Tom Schantz
Married Erin Brownell
One son, one daughter

Andrew Tyler Schantz
February 11, 1989

Chelsie Lyn King
August 17, 1993

Nicole Zahour Schiek
December 7, 1983
Married Josiah Schieck
One daughter

Married Ann M. Bigatel
April 29, 1990

Married James King
1992– 2007, divorced

Thomas Lee Schantz
June 18, 1961, adopted
Three Children

Connie Lynn Schantz
July 26, 1963, adopted
Two Children

Married
August 30, 1953
Two Children

Daniel Wilbur Schantz
March 29, 1934 -
Rosedale, PA

Mildred C. Geissinger
May 29, 1932—
Quakertown , PA

Mary Alice (Schantz)
Conrad
1937 -

Isaac Geissinger
1923-2000

Ada (Geissinger)
Rosenberger
1924—

Ruth (Geissinger)
Longacre
1929-1979

Married 1931
Two children

Married 1922
Four Children

Erwin M. Schantz
1907– 1980
Spinnerstown, PA

Esther M. Longacre
1908-2008
Rosedale, PA

Clarence L. Geissinger
1899-1976
Milford Township, PA

Magdalena Clemmer
1899-1978
Harleysville, PA

The Ancestral Heritage of Dan and Mildred Schantz

Geissinger(Gissinger)/Clemmer(Klemmer)

Mildred's Ancestry

Mildred's Geissinger family heritage can be traced back ten generations to **Jakob Gissinger** of Goetzis, Vorarlberg, Austria. In 1727, the third generation of the Geissinger family immigrated to America on the "Adventure" and settled, on a 372 acre tract of land purchased from William Allen in Upper Saucon. Through marriages and purchases of farm properties in the region, the families settled to farm land in rural Upper Bucks County. In 1847, Philip Geissinger donated the land on which Swamp Mennonite Church was built. Through the next six generations the Geissinger family continued to farm in the region of Upper Bucks County and continued to worship at Swamp Mennonite church. Clarence Geissinger, Mildred's father, would marry Maggie Clemmer, a Mennonite from Harleysville, whose family is also rooted in the early European Mennonite lineage.

Mildred's mother's family descended from **Henry Clemmer**. Henry and his brother John arrived in Philadelphia in 1717 (other sources suggest it may have been 1730) with a group of Mennonite immigrants. His European roots can be traced back two centuries to forebears (Klemmer) who were farmers living in the villages on the Rhine near Cologne. Henry Clemmer settled in Franconia Township, Montgomery (then Philadelphia) County, Pennsylvania as early as 1738. He became a part of the Salford Mennonite congregation. A 156 acre tract of land on Allentown Road south of Franconia was deeded to him in 1748.

Schantz(Tchantz)/Longacre (Longenecker)

Daniels's Ancestry

Daniel is the ninth generation of the **Christian Schantz** family with roots in Europe. Christian Tchantz, was from Bern, Switzerland. His son Kilian moved the family to Asswieler, Germany. His son, Johann Abraham Schantz born in 1745, a devout Lutheran from Assweiler, Germany, immigrated to America and settled in Finland PA. The family remained in the Bucks County and Lehigh County area.

Daniel's mother, Esther Longacre Schantz, was a descendent of Rev. Daniel Longenecker. The family can trace its roots back to the Langeneggers who were recorded in the early 1500's as farmers from the Canton Bern region of Switzerland. **Rev. Daniel Longenecker** immigrated to United States bout 1716. He is recorded to have purchased 220-240 acres from the Penn brothers in 1719. This land is near Royersford, north of Phoenixville. A preacher and a blacksmith, Daniel Longenecker is one of fifteen Mennonite minsters to accept the Dordrecht Confession of Faith in 1727 at Conestoga, Pennsylvania.

Commitment to Faith

Swamp Mennonite Church, Quakertown PA

There are few Sunday mornings that Dan and Mildred cannot be found in their home church, Swamp Mennonite Church on Rosedale Road in Quakertown, PA. Attending Worship and Sunday School has been and will always be a high priority for this Christian couple. Vacations and trips are most often planned so that they would be home on Sunday morning. For Dan and Mildred, it is not enough to simply attend church; to "warm the same pew" each Sunday, since young adults, they have embraced the call to be servant leaders at Swamp Mennonite. Committee service, teaching children in Sunday School and VBS, participating in activities, providing the support and the funding for projects, stewardship of the facility and working in the kitchen or where needed with joy and integrity and the belief that God's

work takes God's people working side-by-side. Theirs is a faith that is unyielding in the belief that God will provide and guide through all of life's circumstances. That God loves His church and will guide the leadership and the congregation through every season.

Swamp Mennonite Church, photo circa 1950's. Men and women entered the church through separate doors.

Dan has served in congregational leadership since he was twenty-one. His teenage experiences as the leader of the youth grew the leadership skills that are his gift. He served the congregation on each of three building committees as the church building was expanded to its current size. He served

1972 Building Committee. Left ot Right:
Dan Schantz, Norman Gehman,
Pastor Winfield Ruth, Horace Longacre,
Isaac Geissinger, Robert Gehman.

as the Building Committee chair in 1991 when the current sanctuary was added. Dan displays a certificate in his office that was presented to him in 2012 marking fifty years of service to the congregation on the Trustee Committee. He continues to oversee the beautiful landscaping of the church grounds. It is a clear example of their stewardship and their love of the visual impact of bedding plants and flowers and expert landscaping. Each Advent season the sanctuary is beautifully enhanced by poinsettia grown in Dan Schantz greenhouses. Christmas Eve is a magnificent display of traditional vibrant red poinsettia. Pots of fresh Lilies adorn the Easter morning services. They are a stunning visual display of the meaning and enhance the congregation's celebration of Easter. At the end of the Christmas Eve and Easter Sunday services these plants are donated through a simple announcement that anyone in the congregation may take one along home with them.

Dan has served as the Cemetery committee chair, on the Finance Committee, on the Church Council; two terms as chairman of the Council. He was instrumental in the establishment of the Mission Outreach committee. He also served on the committee for many years.

Dan and Mildred are enthusiastic supporters of the Youth and their programs. Dan volunteers as the auctioneer when needed and skillfully has taken the honor of Checker Tournament champion. Vacation Bible School closing picnic was run by Dan and Mildred for years. Volunteers reported to the kitchen and Mildred had a task to do and very clear directions. Everything was carefully organized, prepared and notes recorded. They fed crowds and made the work seem effortless. And to work with Dan and Mildred was fun work and always a time of laughter. Mildred's notes and recipe quantities are still used today.

Mildred was the first woman appointed by board and congregation approval to serve on the Church Council. The Church Council along with the elders served as the governing body of the congregation. The Council saw to the oversight and coordinating of the programs and the facility. Mildred also served as the secretary of the council. The council is made up of members who have been asked to consider serving by the Gift Discernment committee prior to Elder approval and congregation endorsement. Mildred has served on this committee many times. She knows the congregation well and she is able to draw out the gifts others have that will serve the congregation and bless them. She has taught young children in Sunday School and Vacation Bible School. She served on the VBS Committee. They planned the entire two week program themselves. Her gift of administration and her desire to help others were evidenced in service on the Helping Hands Committee. She served on the Fellowship and often served in the kitchen. Mildred quips, "I never served as song leader!"

The over 60 New Year's Eve Party was a time for good food, fun and fellowship.

The over 60 Fellowship New Year's Eve gathering was an open invitation from Dan and Mildred to join them at their home. Mildred and Dan prepared spreads of delicious food served on beautifully clothed and decorated tables and hosted games and fellowship. They have a gift of hospitality. It was always there concern that everyone had a good time. More recently they have hosted the group by taking them out to a restaurant for dinner rather than a home cooked meal.

Tithing

D an and Mildred believe that everything belongs to God. They live simply and practice stewardship in every aspect of their lives. Their ability to give generously and cheerfully to their local church and a number of other Christian organizations and missions is the motivation to push to do better financially each year. "The more money I make, the more I have to give," Dan will share. He finds it difficult to talk about. He had been "always taught not to talk about what you did." Sharing in terms of how the next generation is taught at the feet of his generation helps to put a reason to speak about their tithing and charitable giving. They have faithfully tithed every year. There were years early in their marriage and business that they borrowed to pay their tithe of their income. Yes, borrowed. And repaid with interest.

Charitable Giving

H ow does a couple sort through the dozens of worthy organizations requesting funds? Dan and Mildred have focused their giving on those organizations who through their ministry strive to produce leaders and spread the Gospel. Dan has served on many committees and boards of these organizations. His business sense and wisdom have been a vital input to encourage stability and grow ministries. Their generous spirit has spurred leaders on to do what others would say was hardly practical or worthwhile. Communities have benefited from their gifts and the quality of life for those in need has been improved. He has been asked and encouraged to put their name to buildings, wings or auditoriums at several of these organizations. He always refused.

Christopher Dock Mennonite High School in Lansdale was the first major contribution. Approached by a friend, Dan and Mildred contributed to the capital campaign when the school bought the land.

Dock Woods Community in Lansdale, PA. Dan served on the committee that began this retirement community and low-income housing program.

Spruce Lake Retreat and Conference Center. Dan and Mildred have a vested interest in this program from its inception in 1963. Dan and Mildred were with the group who first surveyed the property and had a vision for a camp and retreat center in the Pocono Mountains near Canadensis, PA. Dan has served on the Board. Their financial commitment and continued encouragement has helped drive the leadership to be faithful to the mission of the camp and grow the ministry.

Quakertown Christian School. Dan served on the Development committee. He and Mildred annually enjoy themselves at the Chicken BBQ and Auction. Their generous contributions of funding, quilts and bedding plants and flowers continue to help make this event a successful fundraiser and community tradition.

MAMA Project. Dan and Mildred traveled to Honduras with a volunteer work group to help with this ministry. Dan served on the board of MAMA and was treasurer. They have volunteered their time and financially to this organization that now includes scholarship programs in Honduras and Haiti and provides materials to Child Survival programs across the world.

Life with God. Dan and Mildred financially support this weekly 30 minute Broadcast that airs on stations in PA, NJ, VA and PR.

Mennonite Central Committee (MCC). Dan and Mildred are contributors to the Meat Cannery program. Each year since 1946, MCC sends out a mobile meat cannery, which MCC workers and volunteers use to preserve hundreds of thousands of cans of meat for communities in need across the globe. The collective efforts of all involved produced over a million pounds of canned turkey, beef, chicken and pork; 476,644 cans were shipped to thirteen countries in 2013/1014.

Dan and Mildred made an investment in a Greyhound bus in the mid 80's. They donated the bus, which they had never actually seen, to MCC. They were told by someone that the bus was spotted it in Texas where MCC had put it to use.

Youth for Christ and other organizations have also been supported by this gracious and generous couple. They have worked hard so that they have more to give. They have always felt that their giving was a private matter. Dan's father instilled in him early on that one must be generous in the gift, but it was to be done quietly and not done with public recognition. They realize the importance of others embracing the community and its needs and desire to encourage others to give. Each as they can. They have always been blessed through their generosity. And they are richly blessed by the friendships that have developed over the years through many of the organizations.

Travel

Dan and Mildred have enjoyed and continue to value getting away from the busy schedules their business demands. A few days, a week, even ten days. But seldom more than two weeks.

As seasoned travelers Dan and Mildred find it easy to share of their adventures across the oceans, on five continents, and across the United States. The stories always include how Dan loves to drive and how they love good food, good music, and the ocean shores off the Atlantic and Pacific and the Rocky Mountains. They have enjoyed good service provided on ships, in hotels, and by waitresses. They never fail to show kindness to fellow travelers and the employees of the travel industry. Those who have traveled with them are quick to say that their main concern always is that everyone is having a good time.

Dan and Mildred took their first vacation to Florida. Traveling in their 1950 Ford they took in attractions and some sightseeing. They often stopped to see vegetable fields and usually found road stand markets. It has added to their travels to explore how others were successfully growing produce or displaying it in markets. They always were on the lookout for new ideas and methods. Driving to Florida would be the kind of trips they would take a number of times in the early years of their marriage. During those years, gasoline was very inexpensive. They remember a "gasoline wars" going on in as they drove south one year. They were able to buy gasoline for as low as thirteen cents a gallon.

Early in their marriage they took their first extended vacation and drove across country in Dan's new red and white 1959 Oldsmobile with Dan's cousin, Ken Longacre and his wife, Cora. Their goal was to see the country and head to the west coast. No reservations were necessary

or made. It was 1959. They drove and stopped along the way when
they felt the day was ended. Motels were a popular place to stay while
traveling in the 50's. Dan and Ken would haggle for a better room
rate and it was often settled on as $10 a night. Cousins who grew up
together, Dan and Kenny were competitive and loved to negotiate the
deal. The young businessmen were never far from the love of the deal,
whatever the goal. They ate well and saw the country that trip. On an
exertion from California to Tijuana, Mexico they attended a bullfight.
Mildred quips, "That was the first and last bullfight for me!" Inspired and
refreshed the work load of the farm and business was briefly lightened
by this three week road trip. Mildred thinks that the total cost for the trip
was just under five hundred dollars.

For about twenty years annual winter golf trips would be taken with
three other couples to islands and warm, sunny locations. They traveled
to St. Martin, the Caribbean, Acapulco, Mexico, Puerto Rico, Dominican
Republic, Hawaii or Palm Springs, California. The men played two
rounds of golf from morning until dinner time. The women only golfed
one round each day. This was time to get away and a time to enjoy the
company of friends.

They took an extensive tour in 1987 with Ken and Cora Longacre.
Their trip started with a flight to London, England. They toured London
for several days before taking the ferry across the English Channel. In
Paris, France, they boarded the Orient Express train. They enjoyed
the elegant overnight accommodations of the train trip to Venice, Italy.
They toured Venice for several days and continued on in a rented car.
They drove through and toured through Italy, Liechtenstein, Germany,
and Switzerland. It was a wonderful trip of memorable times with
friends; seeing much of Europe.

Dan and Mildred had been in Europe on two occasions prior to this
trip. They toured and visited Holland, the Netherlands. Both times they
had the privilege of having their bulb salesmen as a tour guide. Each
made sure that they were given access to see the flowers on the main
floor area of the Aalsmeer Flower Auction, a place at the Auction where
only buyers or sellers can go. It is an area that is not visible to the
tourists who view only from above the auction floor. Today Aalsmeer

continues to be the world's largest trading center for plants and flowers. Their salesmen are the ones from whom millions of bulbs; Tulips, Hyacinths, Daffodils and many other varieties are purchased for the greenhouse operation.

Other European trips took them with tour groups to the Passion Play in Oberammergua, Bavaria, Germany. The tour took them through Germany and Switzerland. Other tour trips took them through Egypt and Israel. On their trip to Egypt and Israel was an interesting trip and they had a good time. They flew to Cairo, Egypt and traveled in the area for several days. They found that the pyramids are amazing. They wondered how they could have been built. As they traveled from Egypt and got closer to Israel their tour bus was led by an armored truck. The truck had soldiers in the back with guns in their hands. The bus, escorted by the armored truck took them to a fenced in strip of "no man's land." Here they had to take all their belongings and leave the bus. They walked across this strip to a waiting bus from Israel. They continued their journey and tour of Israel from there.

Their favorite tour trips were to the North Western States and the five trips to the Canadian Rockies. On two separate trips they flew to Vancouver, Canada. One trip they ferried across to Victoria to see Butchart Gardens. A sea plane trip took them back to the mainland and a station to board a train to take them to Jasper National Park in the Canadian Rockies. After  touring Bann, Alberta and Lake Louise they returned to Calgary. They experienced the stampeded at Calgary before flying home. Their second Canadian tour took them by train across the Rockies on the Mountaineer Train. This train would stop at night; they would stay in a hotel. Their meals were taken on the train. Always delicious and quite elegant. Tours of the Northwestern States were taken on motor coach.

The last fifteen years of travel Dan and Mildred have enjoyed cruises. They find it an easy way to travel. They love the convenience of your luggage being taken to your state room. You unpack and do not need repack until the last day of the cruise. Their experiences on cruises have always found the service good, the food delicious and the accommodations great. Having done more than twenty cruises over the years they are experienced. Their cruises have taken them through the Caribbean seas, through the Panama Canal twice, south along the California coast into Mexico, across the Pacific to the Hawaiian Islands, from Barcelona, Spain across the Mediterranean Sea stopping in Rome and visiting the Vatican and other Ports along the way. Copenhagen, Denmark to the Baltic Sea to Sweden, Norway, Germany and as far north as St Petersburg, Russia. They have taken cruises and combination

cruise coach tours to Alaska. They boarded a ship in New York and cruised south along the eastern side of North and South America, Buenos Aires, Argentina. On another South American trip they went to Chile where they hired a tour guide to show them lush fruit growing areas. They then boarded a ship and toured the western side, around the tip of South America and up the eastern side of the continent. They flew home from Rio De Janeiro, Brazil.

Dan and Mildred enjoy music concerts and shows. They have found that time spent in Branson, MO is an enjoyable place to get away and relax. This entertainment town grew up in the middle of nowhere. It is now a busy tourist area with 37 motels and hotels and more than 100 different family shows. They have found a little something for everyone in Branson; country music, magic, comedy, acrobats, horses, violinists, vocal groups, and gospel. Over the last fifteen years they have gone to Branson once sometimes twice a year. One trip during the summer and then again in November for the Christmas shows. They fly out Monday morning, rent a car and attend their first show Monday night. They schedule three shows a day for the next four days and fly home on Saturday. A very full week of entertainment! They have made the trip by car. Driven to Pigeon Forge, TN on to Nashville and then on to Branson, MO.

Dan and Mildred checking out a produce display along the way while on vacation.

If Dan spotted a tomato field along the way while traveling, they had to stop to see how the plants were doing.

While trips have taken them around the globe, they find a day away just as enjoyable. They often take a day away to Lancaster County to visit produce auctions, the outlets and eat in favorite restaurants. A favorite one day excursion is to attend dinner shows. Always a matinee, "the evening shows are too late for us," quips Mildred. Their favorite theaters are in Hunterdon Hills, NJ; The Rainbow Dinner Theater in Paradise, PA and the Dutch Apple Theater in Lancaster, PA.

Part Two

"We live by faith, not by sight."
II Corinthians 4:7

Dan & Mildred Schantz
Business Timeline 1953-2014

1953	o Contracts with Campbell's Soup, Camden, NJ; Conti Tomatoes (plum tomatoes), Brooklyn NY; and Kaplan & Zubrin (green tomatoes), Camden NJ. (75 acres) o Farmed 150 acre on rented fields; Koons Farm, Nace Farm, Links Farm, Schantz Farm (Dan's parents) and Alan Schantz Farm (Dan's grandfather). Grew tomatoes, corn, beans, peas, hay, straw, raised steers, pigs and ducks o Quakertown Auction - outside seasonal produce sales in the midway
1954	o Opened indoor stand at Allentown Fairgrounds Farmers Market; sold produce o Hired migrant laborers through the PA Farmer's Association in Hamburg, PA o Huckster Route, East Allentown – summer produce sales + eggs o Allentown Fairgrounds Market midway. Produce sold late on Saturdays at sellout market
1955	o Bought Christmas trees to be cut down and sold. All sizes. Trees were from farm along route 61 north of Hamburg, PA. Dan bought all the farm had.
1957	o Hired first full time employee, Robert Gehman o Added Gilbertsville Farm Market @ Zern's Market o Purchased Quakertown Road stand building, located building on 320 South West End Blvd., Quakertown on rented land from Edge Brothers (current Pizza Hut location) o Began using day labor crews from Philadelphia. Crew boss (PA State approved) was hired for the day. He arranged transportation and oversaw the crew. The crew boss was paid at the end of the work day and he pays each of the crew. Continue to use labor crews today. o Purchased farm property; 1825 Spinnerstown Road, Zionsville, PA; 96 acres o Farmed over 300 acres (own farm property + additional acreage) o Converted outbuildings to labor camp o Added laying chickens to the business operation

1958	o Opened poultry stand in the Allentown Fairgrounds Farmers Market's new addition –sold dressed chickens, chicken parts, BBQ Chicken and eggs o Quakertown Auction – Leased a space and opened an inside stand ~ sold dressed chickens, chicken parts, BBQ Chicken and eggs o Added bedding plants, flowers, gourds, pumpkins to product line
Early 60's	o Renovated Barn (3 floors) o Built 40'X 315' chicken house. Increased flock to 17,000 layers (Barn held 7,000 layers. Chicken house held 10,000 layers) o Built house for laborers. Building held up to 48 men. It was met PA State guidelines and was inspected randomly throughout the year. They furnished the living quarters and provided food, linens and toiletries. o Grew cantaloupes. Dan pioneered a method of growing them on plastic. The fruit grow faster and the soil retains more moisture. Today this is the standard method for growing vine crops in the field.
1961	o 22' X 100' Greenhouse built (Greenhouse #1)
1962	o Dan was presented with the Quakertown Kiwanis Outstanding Young Farmer Award.
1963	o Greenhouse #2 Built. o Planted orchards of apple (10 acres), peach trees (15 acres), and sweet cherries (1 acre). Added acreage of strawberries (30 acres) red & black raspberries (6 acres), asparagus (5acres), fresh market tomatoes (5 acres), sweet corn (160 acres), 115 acres of mixed produce varieties such as, peas, beans, cucumbers, peppers and 50 acres of canning tomatoes
1964	o Purchased property at 600 State Road, Emmaus, PA. The land needed to be back filled before construction could be done.
1967	o State Road, Emmaus Road Side Farm Market opened. o Total of 19 individual greenhouses @ Spinnerstown Farm o Holiday Fruit Baskets added to product line. Very popular item.

1968	o Dan graduated from Reisch American School of Auctioneering, Mason City, Iowa; Dan was interested in having a license and thought about an auto auction venture. o Fire at Farm property o Hired Joyce Heilman as first secretary. The business office was then located in an enclosed porch at the farmhouse in Spinnerstown. o Purchased and operated Garage business and equipment in Zion Hill, PA
1969	o Began sales at Perkiomenville Auction. Early April through June on Monday Mornings. Sold plants and flowers. o First Flower Show at Ag Hall, Allentown Fairgrounds o Mall sales began; First stand was a Kiosk at Whitehall Mall, Whitehall PA
Early 70's	o Discontinued retail layer and poultry business. Allentown Fairground Market retail interests were sold to Stanley Geissinger o Additional Roadside tents and Mall Kiosks for Holiday Sales (continued through 1980's) MacDade Mall, Holmes, PA; Westgate Mall, Bethlehem PA; Horsham Mall, Stroudsburg Mall; Whitehall, Mall, Montgomeryville Mall, Willow Grove Mall, King of Prussia Mall, Oxford Valley Mall, Pottsville Mall (longest running), Lehigh Valley Mall, Richland Mall, Wyoming Valley Mall and others roadside locations.
1970	o Flower Show at Allentown Fairgrounds Ag Hall o Moon Dust Exhibit at Flower Show. Heavy security required o Held first Antique show in October, "Great Eastern Antique Show and Sale." Memorabilia shows and flea markets were added under the business name of Great Eastern Productions. Daughter, Connie Schantz is a partner. Shows expanded to four times per year.
1973	o Horsham Store Retail Gift Shop with fresh, dried and silk flowers. Open two years. o Sold Christmas trees on lot of vacant A&P store, 2102 Union Blvd. Location would be purchased and a Market opened in 1974 o Office moved from farmhouse to new building adjacent to house.

1974	o Plover Construction Company formed. o Expanded Emmaus Market to a 12 month operation. Bakery added to the facility. Fresh baked pies quickly became a popular item at the market. o Opened East Allentown Farm Market store as Dan Schantz Farmer's Market, 2102 Union Blvd, Allentown PA. Included Vendor stands owned by: Longacre Chicken and Spring Glen Foods, pretzel stand, deli, bakery and a large greenhouse. Nursery plants added to product line
1976	o Antique Show at the Philadelphia Convention Center. 600 vendors including one from England. Show was not well attended because of its conflict with the Flyers' Stanley Cup Finals. o First Year at Lehigh Valley Mall, display and stand in center of Mall
1978	o Opened 675 State Road (Lehigh Street Barn Market), Allentown ; converted 600 State Road property to strip mall o Weekly TV ads on WFMZ, Channel 69. o "Dan's Favorite Family Recipes," cookbook published.
Early 80's	o Hydroponic Lettuce growing system installed. Grew aand sold Butter Crunch head lettuce. Sold well at the retail locations.
1981	o Church View Estates Residential Land developed as residential building lots that were 1.14 to 1.92 acres; 37 lots were up for auction on August 18, 1981. Purchased from P. Hunsberger several years prior.
1982	o Emmaus Market added "Dan Schantz Seafood," and an information booth where customers could pick up free recipes, manufacturers coupon specials and ask questions o Sold produce stand at Allentown Farmer's Market. Closed in January of 1983
1983	o Lehigh Street Market becomes "Dan Schantz IGA Farm Market." Store included IGA Groceries.
1986	o Opened Dan Schantz Market Store, 2525 Easton Ave., Bethlehem, PA

1987	o February 7. Fire at State Road Emmaus Retail Green house. o Dan honored with Mid-Atlantic Master Farmer award. o Sold three farm market locations. o Acquired 15 year lease on the Garden Center at the Big Barn store. o Focused on expansion of wholesale business based on Spinnerstown Road property. No longer produced any edible items. o Began relationship with Walmart stores as seasonal plants vendor o Mall and Tent sales were continued as retail, seasonal locations
1988	o Formed development partnership with Jeff Trainer o "Nature's Nectar" Fruit Basket shop opened at 4th and Susquehanna Streets in Allentown. First retail venture of new partnership with Jeff Trainer. Dan, Jeff, John Carl and Brad DeHoff were the store owners. John managed the store. o Union Blvd., Allentown property developed into strip mall o Appointed by the PA Secretary of Agriculture Dan was approved by the Governor to serve on PA Vegetable and Marketing Advisory Council; an advisory unit of the state agriculture department. Dan was the chairman for ten years. Dan was the only person remaining person from original council when he resigned in 2008.
1989	o Development partnership purchased Traub Market property in Allentown. Developed property into strip mall o Grew fall product line in Farmington, New Mexico (2 years). 1500 acres of gourds, pumpkins and Indian corn
1991	o Mildred wrote "Gardening Tips" A weekly Morning Call column featuring advice for the home gardener and gardening product information and use.
1992	o Ownership of Dan Schantz Farm and Greenhouse became a partnership. Dan offered Patrick Flanley, a longtime employee, 25% partnership. (Dan Schantz 75%, Patrick Flanley 25%)
1994	o Expanded wholesale facilities and operation at Spinnerstown Road property. o Computer controlled (ARGUS) technology ECHO systems and Ebb &Flo floors added to growing sections o New Head House (Shipping and receiving) o Soil and planting rooms added. House Automated planting system and office mezzanine o Seeding and fogging rooms added. o Heating system for the gutter connected greenhouses (102,000 gallon oil tank + boilers)

1995	o Constructed three Refrigerated Cooler rooms (bulb storage) connected to greenhouse and shipping area
1996	o Greenhouse expansion o Painted pumpkins added to product line o Son, Tom Schantz, became part owner (24%) of Dan Schantz Farm and Greenhouses o Character mums added to product line
1998	o Greenhouse expansion o Expanded and renovated Sales and Administrative offices o Network and phone system expanded adding lines to the greenhouse mezzanine offices
1999	o Constructed 3.5 acre Greenhouse complex along Old Bethlehem Pike, Quakertown. Land lease agreement for the site property.
2000	o Greenhouse expansion, a glass open roof structure o Partnership with P & S Development. Development of Lourdes Valley property and Penn Center in Hamlin, PA. Bowling alley and Strip Mall built. o Development partnership purchased land and developed shopping center in Brodheadsville, PA
2001	o "Greenhouse Grower" Top 100 Growers list #67 o Development Partnership approved to build arena on the site of the former Hess's Department Store in Allentown, PA.
2002	o Ownership and business structure changes to Dan Schantz Farm and Greenhouse, LLC. o Tom Schantz sold back his ownership interests. o Seven longtime employees purchase 45% ownership in newly formed. LLC. o Total of 9 ownership partners. Daniel Schantz, Patrick Flanley, John Carl, Nevin Davis, Cynthia Eckenrode, Paul Hardiman,; Dennis Heilman, Lisa Myers, Stephen Thomas. o Grand Opening on September 12 of Dan Schantz Greenhouse and Cut Flower outlet, 2031 29th Street, Allentown. o Named Walmart's "Supplier of the Year." o Discontinued Mall sales and closed Garden Center on State Road, Tent sales continued

2003	o Steel Ice Center, Bethlehem opened. Managed by son, Tom Schantz o Purchased Lehigh Parkway East property for development into high end apartments. o Hickory Hills Estates, Bath PA. The settlement for the purchase and turn around sale of the mobile home park was the same day.
2004	o "Greenhouse Grower"Top 100 Growers list #70 o Purchased Devonshire Towers office complex in Allentown, PA
2005	o Opened second Dan Schantz Greenhouse and Cut Flower outlet at 2100 West Union Blvd, Bethlehem PA o PathMark Supermarket Show, "The Best Booth" in Floral category o Dan received Pennsylvania Vegetable Growers Association Life Membership Annual Award
2006	o Development partnership purchased land in Bethlehem at Stoke Park and Highland Ave. A third party developed and built 55+ Condominiums on the land. Sold land in 2012. o Partnership purchased land on San Antonia, TX Riverwalk. Intended for the development of the Bell South Headquarters. Deal fell through when ATT/ Bell South merger was not allowed by FCC. Bell South Headquarters remained in Atlanta GA.
2007	o Feature article in April, "Lehigh Valley Magazine." Dan was interviewed by Bobby Gunther Walsh
2008	o Leased property in Rising Sun, Maryland. 10 acres of greenhouses and shipping buildings. o Walmart Supplier Award of Excellence
2010	o Purchased Pipersville property. This location includes greenhouses, shipping buildings and offices (11.5 acres). The property includes a home and 60 acres of land.
2011	o "Greenhouse Grower," managing editor, Keith Yanik describes Dan Schantz Farm and Greenhouses as the "Willy Wonka and the Chocolate Factory" of painted pumpkins o Closed Bethlehem Greenhouse and Cut Flower Outlet location

2012	o First year in 45 years to have only one retail location for Easter sales o Dan and Mildred sell their share of the business partnership to longtime partner/employee Patrick Flanley. Dan Schantz Farm and Greenhouse, LLC is restructured. Dan employed by partnership to assist in leadership transition.
2013	o Greenhouse Grower Top 100. Dan Schantz Farm ranked #30. 1,814,381 square feet of environmentally controlled greenhouse space. o Chit-Chat cuties, Paint-Me-Up Pumpkins and Sticker-Me-Up Pumpkins added to Fall wholesale product line o PA Poinsettia Trial and Open House event at Spinnerstown Farm
2014	o Dan Schantz Farm and Greenhouses employing 730 staff during the busy spring season. This includes employees at five locations. o Additional staff is employed to care for the plants at Lowes and Walmart. o Primary bedding plant supplier for Walmart and Lowes o Ranked #31 of the Greenhouse Grower Top One 100. #1 in Pennsylvania. o The greenhouses and fall ornamentals now generate a total gross sales of nearly 40 million annually.

The Early Years

W hile American farmers
continued to dwindle in
number during the 1950's,
in part due to the years of severe drought
and to a changing post War economy, Dan
and Mildred would not be swayed from their
vision to be produce farmers. Dan Schantz,
with his wife by his side, would be numbered
among the thirty-eight percent of the late
50's population of American farmers who
were Mennonite. Dan became known in the
Lehigh Valley and Upper Bucks County region as a skilled produce farmer
and "agri-businessman." He sold at the peak of freshness. Ready to eat.
IIe and Mildred began their business based on trust; in each other, in the
quality of their product and in above all in God's unfailing provision.

Between 1950 and 1960 total farm production output rose twenty-
three percent. American Mennonites farmers significantly contributed
to this increase using the method of farming by means of a systematic
rotation of crops. This natural method of maintaining fertility was also
supplemented by the use of domestic and commercialized fertilizers.
By the 1950s commercial brands of fertilizers were used in addition to
lime and manure. Thus Mennonites have had a reputation of being good
farmers because they preserved the productive capacity of their soils
for centuries on end. This is one reason why farms were kept in single
families for as many as six or seven generations. Dan and Mildred are
keenly aware of the advancements and changes in farming. They tried
new methods. They also trusted in what had worked successfully for
generations on the fields their families had worked. Not every venture
would be profitable. But every venture taught them vital lessons on
building a successful business.

In 1953 the marriage of Dan and Mildred Schantz was the beginning
of a business partnership. Making use of their shared knowledge, hard
work and tenacity the joint ventures began. The business was based on
what Dan had established as a High School student. The fields were rented

in five locations and the crop and equipment were stored at Dan's parents' farms near their apartment. Here they also raised chickens, ducks, pigs and steers. This hardworking young couple had a strong start and deep commitment to each other. Mildred continued her full time job at Longacre Poultry. She would help in the fields and markets in the evenings and on Saturday. There was much work to do. They needed to be able to hire help. There was also a need to grow their business. They needed to find new markets to make their crops easily available to customers. They wanted to expand their product line. They would do all of that.

Huckster Route

Dan hired his cousin and good friend, Henry Gehman, in the early 50's to develop a Huckster route. They were just nineteen. For Henry this was a summer job while attending Goshen College. For Dan, it was a way to extend the summer sales of his produce business. He wanted to take the product to the customer. Dan purchased a route and a truck and worked an area of East Allentown to sell produce and eggs. Hucksters routes were common at this time. Moms at home rarely had their own car to run to the market. Dan and Henry brought the market to them. They sold produce door-to door two days a week. It was hot and often unpleasant to approach some of the customers, but they did well. They enjoyed the challenge. What wasn't sold by Saturday night Dan would take to the Allentown Fairgrounds Farmers' Market. Here they needed a spot to sell out their produce. There was a produce man from Philadelphia who was often anxious to get home. Negotiating a price for the lot of his produce, Dan and the stand owner did the haggling by each of them writing their offer on brown paper bags, Dan would buy him out, and continue selling out. Saturday night's at the Allentown Farmer's Market is where Dan believes he really learned to be successful at the "sell out" deal. Dan and Henry both will say, "We did a lot of yelling." They enjoyed it.

Although Dan continued to sell door to door for a brief time before selling the huckster route, Mildred would not. She asserts that, "Soon after we were married, we had sweet corn. Dan wanted to go door to door to sell this corn. I reluctantly went along, but I refused to get out of the truck."

Early Market Sales

Mildred's first adventure in selling produce was at the Quakertown Farmers' Market in 1954. It was then known as the Quakertown Auction. They had a good sized crop of fresh-picked peas that needed to be sold. Dan took some, and sent Mildred to the Quakertown Auction where she set up a stand in the outdoor midway to sell them. Mildred can still remember that day early in their marriage. She was all by herself doing something she had never done before. She admits she was scared. As far as either of them can recall, she sold all the peas. Dan knew she would. That Saturday would be the first of many years of going to market to sell produce.

The Quakertown Auction opened in 1932 as a large barn with a variety of vendors selling food and all kinds of household goods. It would open on a Saturday afternoon and stay open until nearly midnight. Seasonally there was an outdoor midway area open to additional vendors. It was known as an auction because that is how much of the merchandise was sold. Customers at the market could find household products, remedies and produce. The auction was also open on another day for cattle and pig sales and on an additional day for just poultry and egg sales.

When Dan and Mildred first started to go to the Quakertown Auction outdoor midway they set up their stand along with many other farmers and hucksters selling produce or whatever goods they had. Dan would be accused of "selling too cheap" by the owner of another produce stand. The stand owner went to the Fairground's Market management to complain and told them they needed to "get rid of Schantz." Dan was too respected a young businessman for that to happen and would remain at the Quakertown Auction for years.

Mildred recalls that the Quakertown Auction, especially the midway, "was about the most entertainment people would get those days." She remembers one auctioneer selling from the back of his truck. He sold all kinds of things; housewares, tools, toys, anything imaginable. He kept it entertaining and people would stand around watching for hours. And she recollects the image of a Native American man dressed in a feather hat.

He had liniments and ointments to sell. His stories and testimonies were entertaining and convinced a lot of people to buy his goods. The Auction was more than a market; it was a meeting place for friends and neighbors. It would soon be open on Fridays and Saturdays.

Dan and Mildred took their best produce to market. Most came right from their fields. As early as 1954 they had two to four migrant workers to assist with the picking of the fruits and vegetables. Strawberries, asparagus, scallions and radishes were the early produce offered at their stand. As the season progressed they had all kinds of beans, cucumbers, tomatoes, sweet corn and cantaloupes as well as other varieties. One of the early years they had a good crop of strawberries from their about two acres of plants. Mildred got a much needed new kitchen refrigerator that season. They sold $5,000.00 worth of berries from that crop.

Strawberries and other berries were not available in the markets year round at this time. The first locally grown strawberries were in much demand as soon as the crops were available. Dan saw the demand and wanted to bring to his customers fresh berries as early in the season as possible. Strawberries in Delaware and south New Jersey were ready before those locally grown. Dan would travel to produce auctions in Princess Anne or Laurel, Delaware and Swedesboro, Vineland or Hightstown, New Jersey to find the best berries available and buy truckloads for their retail market stands.

One Saturday Dan showed up at the stand at the auction with a truckload of 320 crates of berries; sixteen quarts per crate. It was late in the afternoon, after three o'clock. And yes, they sold out quickly on that Saturday. After their own fields were done producing berries, Dan would head north to Wilkes-Barre and to Higgins, Pennsylvania to bring berries to their markets from farms that had a later season.

Watermelon was a popular summer fruit enjoyed in July and August by many in those days. At the Auction there were often three or four hucksters selling straight tractor trailer loads of watermelon. A straight load is a truck that is carrying a cargo of one item, watermelon in this case. They would unload them right onto the ground behind their trucks. They usually sold them all. Dan with his helpers sold straight loads of watermelons, potatoes and cantaloupes.

*Dan checks a wagon load of melons for
sale at the auction in Eaton, NC*

They grew what they sold with the addition of the straight loads
of produce Dan was buying at the wholesale markets in Dock Street
Philadelphia, New Jersey and the Carolinas. Most often they had
truckloads of watermelons, potatoes or cantaloupes to sell. Trips to
the Eaton, North Carolina were made to purchase cantaloupe and
watermelon. They always hurried to meet the ferry to cross the
Chesapeake. The tunnel and bridge were not yet built. If they missed
the ferry on the way down it meant waiting for hours for next one and
getting back late for the best part of the auction sales day. If they missed
the ferry on the way back it meant sitting with a truck load ripe fruit that
Dan wanted to get to his customers.

This was a time for honing his skills in buying and selling. One trip
during these early days of retail marketing, he came across a straight load
of vine ripened cantaloupes at the Dock Street produce market in Philly.
The cantaloupes were ripe and ready for the eating, at their peak flavor.
It was a seven or eight ton load. The deal was the whole load. Dan took
the deal. He says he "couldn't resist the opportunity." Mildred could
scarcely believe her eyes when she saw the load coming up the pike from
their apartment window. She wondered, "What's he doing now?" They
sold all of them. Dan knew that with hard work and effort, things could
be done. He had growing confidence and the courage it would take to be
successful as a produce farmer and retailer.

Dan spotted a produce road stand for sale along 309 near Souderton on one of those trips to Dock Street market. The thirty by fifty foot shed with a small overhang would be the humble beginnings of expanding their market. The purchased stand was loaded on two flatbed wagons pulled by a tractor and moved to a location on rented lot along 309 in Quakertown where today stands a Pizza Hut. They hired Ginny Bauder, a young neighbor girl, as their first full time seasonal employee to work at the stand and would later become the manager of the stand. Any leftover perishable produce at the close of sales on Saturday was brought to the stand at the Quakertown Auction and sold. Though small and restricted to seasonal use, Dan and Mildred were pleased with the amount of business they did there.

Dream Farm

Much of their capital during these early years of their marriage would be invested back into the business for the purchase of farm machinery equipment and supplies. Dan and Mildred longed to be able to purchase their own farm property but the funds were low. They were continually investing in the next season. To help make ends meet in the winter of 1954, Dan took a night job in a Hosiery Mill. After nearly four years of saving every penny they could and operating their growing business from their apartment home on Old Bethlehem Pike in Quakertown, they found their dream farm in the spring of 1957. Located in Lower Milford Township, Lehigh County the 96 acre farm was being sold for $24,000. They approached Dan's grandfather, Henry Longacre, for $2,000 in down money. Though he believed the cost of the farm property was steep, he consented to lend them the needed money. They would pay him back, with interest. At twenty-three Dan was able to get an unsecured loan from the bank for the balance. Their signature was all they needed for the mortgage. Dan is still grateful today for that local bank president who had enough confidence in him to approve the loan. It would be another lesson in trust, confidence and business dealings for Dan and Mildred.

The farm property was in need of their immediate attention. Some saw disrepair and neglect. They saw the potential of productive fields. The land had not been farmed for years and was in need of tending.

They envisioned it being restored to its prior layout of neat contour strips to avoid erosion. The structurally sound barn and out buildings also showed signs of inattention, they had a vision for a large chicken house and building a greenhouse for year round production. The farmhouse fortunately was in good order and had had some recent renovations. There was plenty of room for the two of them on the first floor of the house. They rented out the second floor and had monthly income to help meet their mortgage payments until 1965. Renovations would be done in 1965 to meet the family needs of Dan and Mildred and their two young children. The farmhouse would remain their home until June, 1990.

When they had moved to the Spinnerstown Road farm property they had expanded the number of acres they farmed. They needed to secure more day labor. A Crew Boss was hired from Philadelphia. He was to arrange for the number of laborers they requested. He provided their transportation and oversaw their work. The Crew Boss was paid at the end of the day. He then paid each laborer their due. The problem was that many days they did not show up. A labor camp was set up in one of the converted out buildings on the farm. Soon a building that would house up to 48 migrant workers was built and state inspected for operation. Dan and Mildred provided the furnishings for the camp as well as food, linens and toiletries. The migrant laborers provided their own cook. Dan and Mildred paid these laborers each Friday. Many of them were anxious to get to the Post Office on a Friday afternoon to mail money to their families. Over the years the migrant workers and day laborers have come from many countries and nationalities. Crew bosses and day laborers are still used today in the greenhouses. Many have returned each year to work for Dan and Mildred.

The early years at the farm were challenging and busy with little time to consider their impressions of this time or the work. They hand planted, picked, packed and shipped their products and got ready for the next season. The odd years in the late 50's brought drought and harsh growing conditions and their yield and crop quality were affected. For a seasonal produce farmer the months of October through February were slow. Mildred would freeze and can their food for the winter. If they had a little money to purchase toilet paper and soap, there needs were met, Dan would say. They never considered giving up. Each year was another that grew their faith in God's constant provision. They stood by their vision of the farm operation supporting a produce business. The farm would grow with them as the business grew and as their family grew. Today the farm property continues to serve as the center of the Dan Schantz Farm, LLC wholesale operation.

Tomato Contracts

Dan and Mildred are experienced tomato growers. Their youthful days had left fond memories of long summer hours spent handpicking 5/8 baskets of tomatoes from Mildred's parents' fields. Their hands had planted the young bare root plants provided by Campbell's Soup Company and Conti Tomatoes. They watched and waited in anticipation of the first fruits of harvest. Their own produce business now had rented fields of almost two hundred acres, fifty acres in tomato production. Dan began his tomato farming with the first two dedicated acres he had while in High School. They needed more help. Isaac, Mildred's brother, was also raising canning tomatoes and had employed the use of migrant laborers. These laborers came from Puerto Rico through the PA Framer's Association. The Association's office was in Hamburg, Pennsylvania. Isaac had a few men in his camp and has space for a few more. Dan and Mildred arranged to hire a few men and began their practice of using migrant workers. In 1957, soon after they had purchased the Spinnerstown farm, they hired their first full-time employee, Robert Gehman. Robert recalls his first few days of work were spent days with Dan covering the tomatoes plants with plastic tents to save them from frost. This back straining task was a new experience for Robert. The tomatoes plants were their market plants for local produce sales. That late spring seventy acres of contract tomato plants froze on May 26, 1957. They had just worked almost day and night to get them planted. They would now need to replant all of them. There were drought years in the late fifties and a year that the rains came at the right time. That year they would have a good bumper crop to harvest and deliver. With the help of migrant laborers the tomatoes were handpicked into baskets that were loaded on wagons from the fields and then full baskets were straight stacked in open bed trucks. There is an art, a skill to stacking straight loads of baskets on a truck. Dan is an expert. He would load the critical bottom row. With three trucks they would have a load on the road to Camden, one being loaded with baskets that were on wagons from the fields and one on a return trip from Camden. The goal was to ship seventy-five loads that season. There was a bonus to Robert if they met the goal, a new hunting rifle. They worked morning until night loading and delivering tomatoes to Campbell's Soup Company in Camden, NJ for six to eight weeks beginning in late August. Robert got his rifle. They, as did many farmers in the area, would continue to grow and deliver tomatoes to the canneries until the early seventies.

Acres of plum tomatoes were grown for Conti tomatoes. Some were delivered to their processing plant in Palm, PA while others were taken to the wholesale market in Brooklyn, NY. The tomatoes for the wholesale market were packed in bushel baskets with lids. The heavy baskets were sold to local Italian home cooks who made their own sauce. These tomatoes got a better price than those sold to the cannery. Green tomatoes picked from the fields were sent to Kaplin & Zubrin tomatoes in Camden, NJ or a vendor in the Brooklyn NY Terminal Market for pickling. These had to be a uniform size and totally green. It was worth the extra effort. They got a good price for them.

For their own markets, acres of tomatoes were also grown or purchased wholesale. In June into early July before their own tomatoes were ready to harvest, Dan would purchase a truck load of green tomatoes in Columbia, SC or St. John's Island, SC. The tomatoes were placed into the refrigerated rooms on the farm. The cooling unit was turned off. A ripening agent was circulated in to the sealed off area. Within a few days the tomatoes would begin to ripen. This is the same process used for most tomatoes sold in markets today. The tomatoes were sorted according to color before being sent to market. They would not be sold until the proper time: tomatoes of good red color and delicious taste.

Growing tomatoes was a high risk crop. Weather played a major roll. Without the use of an irrigation system there yield was weather-dependent. If the summer brought too much rain and cool weather it could cause the crop to be infested with blight or other diseases on the other hand a dry summer could cause dry root. Apart from the weather conditions, there would also be the stress of getting the crop picked and delivered on time to the cannery. Crew leaders would promise a picking crew and then not show up. This was all part of the canning tomato business. Growing tomatoes also had its good and rewarding years. It was a good source of income, a cash crop that Dan and Mildred knew they would receive the much-needed check on schedule as per their contract. Dan and Mildred will always be grateful to Clarence and Harold Rosenberger, owners of Clover Leaf Mill, who allowed them to carry and grow their chicken feed and fertilizer bill all through the summer. Dan and Mildred always paid this bill first when the check came from the Campbell's soup company. Mildred to this day doesn't recall ever being late paying off a note or mortgage. If they borrowed from family members, they always paid back, with interest.

Today seventy-five varieties of tomato plants are grown by partner Steve Thomas as an annual trial of varieties to determine which will be grown in the greenhouse the next year. The very best of the trial is named "Dan's Favorite." It is always a best seller in their retail market.

Photos circa mid-1950's. Tomatoes stacked loaded and redy for delivery near their Koon's apartment in Quakertown. Photo on the bottom right shows trucks waiting to deliver their load of tomatoes at the Campbell's facility in Camden, NJ.

Poultry Business

S oon after the farm was purchased the barn renovations were done. The barn was now a three story structure that partially was used to house and expand their layer flock. Additionally, a large 315' X 40' chicken house was added. Dan went to a lumber liquidation auction to purchase the materials needed to build this sizable structure. He

The chicken house on a sunny day at the Spinnerstown Farm.

bought the exterior and interior plywood, nails, thermopane windows and just about everything they needed. It was a state of the art design for the early 60's. The structure was built with trusses using insulation between the interior and exterior plywood. The raised, slatted floor was over a large pit for the droppings. This would be cleaned out after each new flock of laying hens. Hens were replaced about every fifteen months. The building had automatic feeders, watering systems and egg collectors. They now had the capacity for a total of 17,000 laying hens. This was a quite sizable operation for the area at that time and illustrative of the changes in poultry farming of the time. The chickens did well, enjoying nice sunshine, through the windows. Though automated, there was still plenty of work to do.

Getting their poultry products ready for weekend markets took a lot of preparation. Chickens as well as ducks, turkeys and sometimes rabbits were dressed each week on Thursdays at Dan's parents' poultry farm. This was the one job that Mildred did not care for as a poultry farmer. They did what needed to be done and worker side-by-side with the hired help. If they did not have enough of their own chickens ready for slaughter, Dan would purchase what was needed; either at the poultry auctions in Harleysville, Fogelsville or Quakertown. Each auction was held on a different day of the week. If one did not have what he needed Dan would go the next day to another location.

After the poultry was prepped and cleaned on Thursday it was put into a vat of Ice water. The next morning it was packed on ice and taken to the markets. They dressed a total of between 350 to 500 each week. The ice was delivered by the ice man from an ice making plant in Quakertown. The plant had freezer drawers that could be rented. This was popular before home freezers became available.

Hundreds of Muscovy ducks were raised on his parent's farm property. Eggs were primarily sold to retail and some wholesale distributors. Retail sales for their chicken, eggs, chicken parts, capons, turkeys and duck were part of their markets stands at the Allentown Fairgrounds Farmers Market and the Quakertown Market. The displays were attractively and precisely done to highlight the best of their poultry and attract buyers. Their neatly arranged stands were known for their displays. The eggs were on the counter piled high, according to size and color, brown and white. The stands at both the Allentown Fairground Famer's Market and at the Quakertown Market included a BBQ machine. This was a fairly new technology and the chicken was well-known, made just right. Chicken scrapple was also made each week and sold at their poultry counters. This was not at first a well-known or popular item of the time, but when their customers purchased it they usually came back for more. With the demands of their expanding produce markets in the mid-60s, Dan and Mildred would determine it was best to sell their poultry business. The Allentown Farmer's Market interest was sold to Stanley Geissinger who had run the stand for them for years.

Poultry stand at the Allentown Fairground's Market.

New Challenges

In business Dan had learned quickly you can never stand still. He and Mildred sought out new markets and products and learned new growing techniques. There were risks and there would be additional hard work. Dan and Mildred would not fear either. They would see what others would doubt the viability of and they would invest in it. Their time. Their produce. Their belief in what God generously had given to them.

The challenge was how to extend the season. They had good field and seasonal market help from the peak months of April through October. They needed to have work for them work during the slow months. The first greenhouse built in 1961 proved to be the solution. The greenhouse was built using Cornell University plans. Using posts and two-by-four trusses the ninety-nine foot structure was wrapped in a double layer of polyurethane. Air was forced through the layers to act as insulation. This meant that bedding plants and flowers, gourds and pumpkins added to the product line would keep everyone working year round. Additional items for markets meant additional income to reinvest into their fast growing produce and plant business. The success of this venture multiplied and greenhouses were added throughout the sixties. They were always looking for more greenhouse room as their expanding product line sold well at wholesale and retail markets. Using the first 22 X 100 foot greenhouse as a model, through the 60's and 70's they would build a total of 42 freestanding greenhouses on their farm property. The demands of their markets and business increased and in 1983 they undertook the construction of gutter connected greenhouses. The location needed to be excavated to level the area. Three gutter connected greenhouses 324' X 210' and a work area of 40' X 420' would serve the business well for a few years. Additional greenhouses were needed. This excavation of the sloping property required a lot of soil to be moved to level the area and prepare the site. They spent over one million dollars just to get ready to build. Connected to the first gutter connected greenhouses, this expansion was the same size as the first, three gutter connected greenhouses 324' X 210' in size. Business growth demands and increases in sales brought Dan and Mildred to make the decision to expand again. Three more gutter connected greenhouses were built.

This brought the total of greenhouse space to ten and a half acres at the farm. Through the next twenty years gutter connected greenhouses were built bringing the total to seventeen and a half acres of greenhouse space at the Spinnerstown farm. Today Dan Schantz Farm and Greenhouses, LLC has 1,814,381 square feet of environmentally controlled greenhouse space. It was ranked 30 in the nation and is number one in Pennsylvania by Greenhouse Grower in 2013.

In addition to greenhouses, orchards of peach and apple trees were added on property in the sixties , as well as acres of red and black raspberries and asparagus. The peaches were a very important addition to the expanding product line. In additional to their own orchard they also rented the orchard of a neighbor for a number of years. Apples were a big part of their fall season. Their orchard and the rented neighbors produced many varieties for their markets. They also made apple cider. This was a popular product from September to Christmas. Dan and Mildred took great pride in choosing the right mix of apples to make the best and sweetest cider. They worked long days. Dan's weekly schedule was to work in the fields until late Thursday and drive that night to the Dock Street markets in Philadelphia to purchase produce beginning at midnight when it opened. He tasted everything. He only bought what was fresh and the tastiest. Not always the cheapest. His passion was to consistently bring the best possible product to consumers at their markets. Friday morning, directly from Dock Street, he drove with his loaded truck to set up at markets. He worked the markets all day on

Allentown Fairgrounds Market Stand, circa mid-1960's
Cantaloupes are 3 for $1.00   Corn is 15 ears for $1.00 and
Green Peppers are 2 for $.29   Peaches are 4 lbs. for $1.00

Friday until they closed at 11 PM. Employees remember how Dan could be heard be yelling at customers, bagging and making change as fast as he could. "Lady, don't touch that!" "Lady, get your purse off there!" Dan chuckles, he knows, "That's what I'm famous for, yelling at the costumers." He particularly did not want them touching every piece of fruit or produce and the displays. A great deal of effort had been put into creating attractive displays. And he did not want to sell bruised produce. It was usually 1 AM on Saturday until he finally went to bed. "Those crazy hours never bothered me then, but now I wonder about my sanity at the time," Dan says with a thoughtful smile. He loved bringing fresh produce to consumers as much as he loved produce farming.

Dan and Mildred were, as Dan put it, "ready to spread their wings a bit further." In 1964 they purchased a piece of property on well-traveled State Road in Emmaus right near the Allentown border where it becomes Lehigh Street. One month later Dan had an offer for a $10,000 profit on the property. He would not sell. His grandfather quipped at a family gathering that he heard "he had a relative that turned down a $10,000 profit." Dan stood by his decision. The land needed to be backfilled before construction could begin on the farm market store. It would be three years until the market doors were open for business. It was an immediate success. Arlene Matkes was the energetic manager of the market. She always did her best to be sure that the market was kept looking good for customers. The sign advertising their new market said, "We grow most everything we sell." Here they had a ready market for their fruits and vegetables as well as plants, flowers, fall ornamentals, homemade preserves and jellies, apple cider in season and fruit baskets.

First roadside market along State Road in Emmaus, PA. Opened in 1967.

Fall products from their orchards. Beautifully displayed and ready for customers at the Emmaus road stand market.

They kept the doors open for 10 months of the year, closing only in January and February. From early bedding plants and Easter flowers potatoes and root vegetables through the Christmas sale of greens and Christmas trees it was a busy market of satisfied customers. Still Dan was not satisfied. If the market proved to be successful for ten months out of the year what would draw customers to the market twelve months of the year? He knew that with the right addition to his product line customers would buy that item and their weekly produce, "Just as hot dogs taste better at a ballpark, fruits and vegetables always seem fresher in a farm market—regardless of the time of year." In 1974, the doors did not shut the doors in January. Dan found his product: fresh baked pies. A bakery with display cases and a walk-in freezer were added and within two days the first pies sales were ready for costumers. The aroma of fresh baked cinnamon buns, breakfast cakes and breads enticed customers to buy. Frozen readymade pies were purchased from Michigan supplier, Chef Pierre, and baked as needed on site. They were delicious.

Customers said they could not tell them from home-baked. And the profitable pies were the popular item that kept the market open year round.

Their markets now would include the State Road Market, produce and poultry at the Allentown Fairgrounds Market, the poultry stand at the Quakertown Farmer's Market and the produce stand at the Gilbertsville Zern's Market. They farmed three hundred acres. These were busy days for Dan and Mildred. They are thankful for the hard work and support of their employees. During one of those busy summer days Dan and Mildred recall having quite a scare. One of their employees was filling a tractor with gasoline. He may have been smoking. The tractor caught fire. The garage attached to the barn burnt down. The fire company was able to save the barn. Still today past and present employees express gratitude for the grace extended and the lessons learned in their employment experiences with Dan and Mildred.

Winters were a much slower pace. Dan took the opportunity in 1968 to attend Reisch American School of Auctioneering in Mason City, Iowa. He became fully licensed. Dan considered ways he would use his auctioneer's license, including the idea of a used car auction. Farming and produce retailing would remain his passion.

In 1969, Dan put his auctioneer's license to use and began selling seasonal plants at the Perkiomenville Auction every Monday for the next forty-two years. He would sell them fast. Six "runners" would deliver the sold plants to the customers and collect their money. Two people would be on the truck and handing him the next plants to be sold. He enjoyed it, but it was hard work. One of the stories Dan likes to tell about his Monday's in Perkiomenville is about his license. No one ever asked if he had a license. That is until one Monday a PA State inspector came through the auction. He stopped Dan's sale and asked Dan

Dan is shown ready to auction off more of their products. The girls in the photo are the "runners," hired for that day's auction, they were ready to deliver the plants to the customers and collect the final sale price.

to show his license. Dan quickly opened his wallet and proudly showed the inspector his license. It made Dan's day.

Most of the car and truck repairs and services for the business were done at a garage along Old Bethlehem Pike in Zion Hill, PA. When the owner wanted to retire, Dan and Mildred purchased the business. They leased the building and hired Cliff Mease, Sr. to operate the business. Truck and auto repairs were the main work done by the employees of the garage. They were licensed to do State inspections and also sold some gasoline. They kept the business for several years before selling it to one of the employees.

Retail sales were going well. During the busy months summer months they retailed over 200 tons (10 trailer loads) of produce each week from their farm crops and also from wholesale purchases. Dan and Mildred sold ninety percent of the crops they grow. Harvests from their fields and stand sales would vary daily. With the installation of walk-in coolers there was minimum waste of unsold, overripe produce. The demand for plants and produce was increasing each season. It was time to focus on their greenhouse business. They sold their poultry and egg stands. The chicken house was rented to a nearby neighbor.

Mildred was doing all of the bookkeeping and office work, working in the greenhouse and going to markets on Fridays and Saturdays. In 1968 they hired a secretary to help lessen the load for Mildred. Joyce recalls those years as happy ones. She was a part of the family as much as an employee. They enclosed the porch on the farm house as the office.

Tent sales and Mall Sales

Left: From 1970's: One of Mildred's hand drawn diagrams showing how a sales tent was to be set up. Right Photo: Mother's Day Sales tent in Allentown ready for customers.

During the late sixties and through the seventies and eighties Easter flower sales were expanded through tent sales at busy roadside locations and at area Malls in kiosks. It was a hectic time. Everything needed to be in bloom on schedule.

The deliveries needed to be on time and to the right place. It was no easy task to have them set up with proper price signage. Mildred gave employees careful instructions. They were grateful for honest employees who manned all the locations. After the tent locations were closed on late Saturday night, many of the location managers would gather at Dan and Mildred's house to count the money. The money was dumped on the dining room table. Each person was assigned what bills they were to count. And those were the only bills you were to touch recall one of the "Schantz team." And they enjoyed an evening of reminiscing about the sales over the previous few days.

Above Left: Tent and Mall sales were hand recorded on pieces of cardstock in spreadsheets.
Above Right: The Easter sales area in Whitehall Mall. Late 70's.

Flower Shows and Antique Shows

In the spring of 1969 Dan and Mildred held their first Flower Show at what was then called the Agricultural Hall (now known as the Agri-Plex) of the Allentown Fairgrounds. This event was a dream of Dan's. Dan and Mildred spent long hours designing and putting together beautiful colorful garden settings. The plants, in full color, were all from their greenhouses. It was a lot of physical work. There was a small pond with a duck slide and waterwheel. The children especially enjoyed watching the trained ducks climb a ladder to get their food, slide back into the water and hurry back up the ladder for more food. Area landscapers and gardening clubs and groups also created garden displays to share their style and inspire homeowners to plan and plant landscaping on their property. Venders set up booths to sell garden equipment and plant related items. Thousands of visitors enjoyed the beautiful show. Plans were immediately made to do a show in the spring of 1970. American astronauts Buzz Aldrin and Neil Armstrong walked on the moon in the summer of 1969. They returned to earth with about 50 pounds of moon dust. Dan felt this would be an added attraction for the flower show and set into motion a plan to display moon dust at the 1970 Flower Show. Arranging for it was not an easy achievement. After many tries and finally making the right request to the right people, Dan and Mildred were permitted to put on display some moon dust. It was to be held under heavy security. A security guard stood next to the display at all times. The moon dust was kept under lock and key at all times. It did create a lot of interest. Though well received by the public, the garden displays had to be worked on until the wee hours of the morning of the show opening to have them all perfected. The third year of the show they worked until 4 AM finishing the displays for the 10 AM opening. Mildred said, "That's enough. I will never do this again regardless of how successful it is." And they never did a flower show again. But, Mildred adds, "This was the birth of our Antique Shows."

Agricultural Hall at the Allentown Fairgrounds was rented and table spaces were sold to antique dealers. The first show with 20 dealers was held in 1970 was known as the "Great Eastern Antique Show and Sale." The show's popularity quickly rose with the public and

Long lines of "treasure seekers" waiting to get into the Memorabilia Show at Ag Hall in Allentown.

with dealers. The two shows each year in Allentown drew large crowds. The Hall could accommodate 156 dealers. It was usually sold out with additional dealers seeking to secure a spot at the popular shows. Dealers would often sell out on the items they brought. They expanded shows to other cities; the Expo Center in Fort Washington, PA; Mid-Hudson Civic Center, Poughkeepsie, NY, the Wilkes Barre Armory in Kingston, PA and Renningers in Kutztown, PA.

Joyce Heilman was the general manager of the shows which continued until the interests were sold in 2013. She was in complete charge of each venue and the event; the advertising, renting stands to dealers, the mailings to attract dealers, organizing the tables and wall backboards. Dan would help on opening day to help with the lines of customers who stood in long lines around the building waiting to get into the show. Memorabilia shows and garage shows/flea markets were added to the business venture in addition to the Antique Show & Sale under the name of "Great Eastern Productions." The company's goal was "to make sure that every customer who walks into the building is treated with warmth and courtesy." This policy helped them to get a loyal customer base who returned year after year. The shows featured the wares of dealers from 11 states, displaying a wide spectrum of antiques; antique baking supplies, antique glassware, jewelry, furniture, dolls, clocks, clothes and more. Some of the more unique shows were the 'Great Eastern U.S. Spring Antique Book, Paper & Advertizing Show' and 'Great Eastern U.S. Summer Antique Book, Paper & Advertizing Show.' These shows showcased pop culture, memorabilia and paper collectibles.

By far the most exciting undertaking of the Great Eastern Productions venture was the show in May of 1976 at the Philadelphia Civic Center. There was great interest to do this size show in the Philadelphia area during the time of many celebrations of our countries 200th birthday. Over three hundred dealers from around the country

── GREAT EASTERN U.S. WINTER──

ANTIQUE SHOW & SALE

December 6, 7, 8, 1985
ALLENTOWN, PA
Agricultural Hall, 17th & Chew, Allentown Fairgrounds

FREE PARKING

HOURS: FRI. NOON-9:30 PM, SAT. 11 AM - 9:30 PM
SUN. 11 AM-6 PM

ADMISSION $2.75

ONLY $2.50 WITH THIS CARD

156 QUALITY DISPLAYS
OVER 100 DIFFERENT THAN THE FALL SHOW!

Postcards were made available to vendors (about 50 to 100) for their booths. The vendors would display them at other shows. The cards were also distributed in the retail markets.

and England rented space. Everything was made ready. The big day came but attendance was very poor. The show was open on the same weekend as the Philadelphia Flyers were playing in the Stanley Cup finals. It was an expensive experience.

Christmas Trees

The Quakertown Route 309 road stand was the site of the first Christmas tree sales in the late 50's. Dan did not have any experience in buying or selling trees but sought out local ones for this first venture. It did not take long to be connected with a tree farm in Berks County, PA north of route 22 along route 61. Dan bought a 55 acre patch. They were cleared to cut everything. The blue spruce ranged in size from 2 feet to 18 feet. Their price was good, but it took a lot of work to get them cut and to their lot to sell. Christmas trees were now part of their retail product line.

The sale of Christmas trees from a vacant parking lot on Union Blvd in Allentown was Dan's idea in 1973. The lot had been used for spring and fall seasonal flower sales. Why not continue seasonal sales from this location? Dan's vision was not to begin to farm his own Christmas trees but rather resell ones purchased from local growers. They would continue to buy local through the time when the trees became too pricey. Dan found a better price for his customers and the Douglas Fir variety that they wanted. The decision was made to supply wholesale markets with trees. The best place to find acres of Douglas Fir was Oregon. A steno notebook bares the records of a tree buying trips made in the late 80's to Oregon. Patrick and Dan traveled in late August to shop for trees for the three store locations. Patrick at this time was the manager of the Union Blvd market in Allentown. He carefully made notes on each of the growers visited and the details of the sales. The quality of the trees was noted. "Somewhat small—but we need them." The directions were given to them by locals. There were no maps or GPS directions, just handwritten notes of the turns and miles to travel in the remote corners of the state.

In the fall of 1989 Dan and Mildred made the Christmas tree buying trip to Oregon. They had the names and addresses of growers, some of whom they had purchased trees from in previous years. The trees look great. They were able to get them for what they thought was a right price. The arrangements all seemed to be in order. Dan and Mildred enjoyed the trip; they toured through some beautiful farming areas and ate dinner in a great restaurant on top of Mt. Hood. The trees arrived and were sold at their markets. Problems with the trees began to be reported back to store personnel. As the trees warmed in the homes of those who purchased them; the needles quickly fell off. They found out that the trees were brought to Pennsylvania on open flatbed trains which passed through regions of freezing temperatures. The native growing area of the trees had never gotten that cold. The trees had frozen but did not show signs of any problems on the sale lots. It was the last time they had trees shipped from Oregon. Today trees are purchased and sold for wholesale customers and for their retail Lehigh Street store. The trees come from Pennsylvania and North Carolina. Frasier Fir is now the popular variety of fresh cut trees for homes and retail displays.

DAN SCHANTZ

FARMERS MARKET
LEHIGH STREET, EMMAUS, PA.
2102 UNION BLVD., ALLENTOWN, PA.

Company Logo. Mid-1970's.

One of the first produce trucks painted with the company logo. 1976.

Retail Markets Expansion

T he vacant lot of the closed A&P grocery store in East Allentown that served them well as a seasonal tent sale location interested Dan and Mildred. The empty grocery store became available for purchase in 1973. Dan describes the move to make the purchase as "an expansion itch." They tore the store completely apart for renovations and put it back together in just two months. Dan did the hiring for the store employees from his car in the parking lot. On the first day for interviews, there was a line a half block long of applicants. Each one was invited to sit in his car for their interview. Many were hired on the spot. In May of 1974, Dan Schantz Farm Market at 2102 Union Boulevard, Allentown PA opened. The store featured beautiful displays of fresh produce. One sign in the store reminder customers just how fresh, "IF YOU CAN FIND FRESHER FRUITS & VEGETABLES – THEY ARE STILL GROWING." There was a good deal of display

space on the store sales floor.
A greenhouse was added
and landscaping shrubbery
was sold in addition to the
bedding flowers, plants and
vegetables. Cut flowers and
arrangements were added
to the sale floor. The store
was a true farmer's market
that included vendor
owned sales stands of

Dan Schantz Farm Market

fresh poultry, fresh meats, salads, fresh fish, a deli counter and a bakery.
Denny Heilman became the first store manager. Dan did the produced
buying for the markets. "There was no one better," Denny shares with
pride. He was amazed at how Dan could remember numbers and details.
"He could tell you what he paid for grapes four weeks ago, but he
couldn't always remember your name." Dan began to host the TV ads
for local stations. Mildred gave oversight to the greenhouse and floral
operations as well as input into the advertising for the business.

The store was not doing well as well as Dan expected. Week after
week for about six or seven weeks, Dan would do a store walk-through;
his retail instincts said there was something wrong. His employees were
not able to sort it out. Dan said it became clear to him as soon as he saw
a photo of the store sales floor. It was then that he immediately knew
what to do and how to change the store layout. That afternoon they
added more displays put together from melon crates and boards. Store
manager, Denny Heilman describes the store sales floor as going from
spacious to jam-packed. It made all the difference in the store sales.
Dan's ability to successfully market produce left an impression on all his
young employees.

Long time employees Patrick Flanley and John Carl also served as
store managers. Dan and Mildred's son Tom Schantz would also be a
store manager of the market.

There was never a time that Dan and Mildred were not considering new ventures in their journey as a couple. In the midst of raising a family, their commitment to their church and their expanding wholesale and retail markets, they formed a construction company; Plover Construction. Nate Heilman was hired to run the company. Nate was in their employ as a facilities manager. He and his crew did a lot of the repairs and general maintenance on their properties. One of their first major undertakings would be the farm office building. Joyce Heilman laughs when she recalls how she and Mildred saw the concrete pad for the building and thought it was giant—they were sure the completed building would be much too big for one secretary. The expanded building continues to serve as the main office for the business where fifteen employees share very cozy office space. The company built several house and also converted the labor camp building into two apartments. The projects were done during a period in the local economy when the interest rates were high and houses, including new construction were hard to sell. The company would be dissolved after several years.

The Big Barn Store. One stop shopping on Lehigh Street in
Allentown was open from 1978 to 1987.

By 1977 the Emmaus Road stand market was outgrown. Parking was not adequate. More retail space was needed. A large car dealer's lot across the street became available for sale. It was big and expensive. Dan and Mildred felt this was a "big bit to chew" but after careful consideration and prayer the decision was made to purchase the property. There was much work to do. Plans were developed and needed to be approved for the building. The market was designed to be a place where customers with one stop shopping. The plans were approved to build a 54,000 square feet building, with an additional 4,000 square feet of greenhouse and garden center. An important factor in the opening of the store was the securing of vendors. Rental commitments needed to be secured in time so everyone was ready for the planned opening of Mother's Day week in 1978. After a lot of work and convincing the concession vendors were secured; Madtes Poultry, Clover Farms Meat, Heagey Quality Delicatessen, Madtes Bulk foods, Zeigler pretzels chips and snack foods, Shaffer's Health Center, Longacre Seafood, Mike's Deli and Sandwich shop. The building needed to be done in the winter. The winter was a cold and snowy one. The finished store was just as Dan had envisioned it. A "one stop shopping " place for their customers. It featured a bakery where Dan Schantz employees baked and sold breakfast cakes, doughnuts, decorated cakes, cinnamon buns and pies. There was a cut flower market for cash and carry fresh bouquets and arrangements, a gift shop with collector items, crystal bowls and vases porcelains, silk and dried flowers, garden crafts and accessories and garden chemicals. The produce department provided the space needed to display and to offer for sale a more complete line of fresh products. They

Greenhouse at the Big Barn Store.

sold all their own grown produce plus everything that was available from many other states and around the world. Their goal was to offer the best and most competitive price which was often much lower than other local grocery stores and markets. They opened the market with a full line of IGA grocery products. In 1983 the "Big Barn Store" grocery department became an IGA supermarket, known as Dan Schantz IGA Farm Market. IGA was their general grocery item supplies with competitive prices and all concessions were now open six days a week, instead of just Wednesday through Saturday. The store greenhouse was always packed with their own plants and flowers. These were grown in their own greenhouse at the Spinnerstown Farm location. The displays were like going to a flower show each season of the year. Terrarium gardens in many sizes and bonsai plants were popular. Their staff was expert at putting custom terrariums together for customers. They used then popular colored sand and pebbles and a great collection of terrarium size plants. Outdoors the garden center provided customers with a large selection of shrubs and flowering shrubs, evergreens, and fruit trees as well as the accessories and mulch the home landscaper needed.

By December of 1982, after being somewhat reluctant to break a thirty year tradition they sold the produce stand in the Allentown Farmer's market. Dan has said, "It was becoming more difficult to maintain an interest there."

Dan's Favorite Family Recipes

Cover of the Cookbook. Many of the reccipes were tested and developed by Dan's mother, Esther Schantz.

Dan had a great deal of respect and admiration for the many good cooks he had been blessed with in his life; two grandmothers, a mother, a mother-in-law and his wife. He thought a cookbook that focused on family recipes using fruit and vegetables should be shared. He quickly learned that many of the family recipes were not in written form, they just "always made it this way." Friends and relatives were willing to share their recipes and offered helpful hints, the real task was to put the recipes in exact measurements, steps and a standard written form. Dan's mother, Esther Schantz, played a key role in the months of work it took to preserve these favorite Pennsylvania Dutch recipes. She spent countless hours cooking foods, writing notes and keeping records of ingredients. Many are from the dishes she made and sold at her family's market stand. The popular cookbook was first published in 1984.

An additional market was opened in 1986 on Easton Avenue in Bethlehem. The converted and expanded the former Gorman's IGA store on the site became the adding third location to the existing markets at

*Full Page Morning Call Ad
from June, 1986.*

2102 Union Blvd. in Allentown and 675 State Road, Emmaus. Their plan was to open a market similar to the Big Barn store on Lehigh Street in Allentown. Patrick Flanley gave oversight to the renovations of the store and became store manager. It did well. It was close enough to their Union Boulevard market to be known by area customers. Advertising was consolidated to one ad each week. All items were now available at all three locations at the same price. Mildred set up the ad tear sheets each week for their Morning call ad.

Dan and Mildred know the value of advertising. It is money well spent in a business. Your customers need to know that your product is the one to purchase and at what price. Is the price better than the competitions? Mildred developed all the ads. Some were flyers to hand out in neighborhoods, mailings or banners. "Mildred's Room" is across from the office. A place where she cut and pasted clip art and hand painted banners and signs for the stores. Mildred added her gardening wisdom to their Morning Call advertising in a weekly "Gardening Tips" feature in 1991.

Venders were different at each market location and did their own advertising. Their retail business was now operating strictly in their own markets. Dan and Mildred were well aware that this was not an easy time to be in business and to stay in business. They describe

This familiar sign could be found at the Emmaus, Bethlehem and East Allentown market locations. Space was rented to private shop owners to make each location a one stop shopping experience. "I would rather concentrate on what I know, and let them sell what they know," Dan said.

this time as "busy, exciting, demanding, rewarding and frustrating." They were diversified enough in their products, markets and business to meet the demands of the 1980's economy. They urged their employees to "look for and plug up leaky holes," and meant it. They did not like waste; wasted time or wasted materials. They were now employing about 150 people in all their business locations and the farm locations

Dan's aim with all his employees was to be available to help each one in some way. Dan has shared this story as part of a speech to let the listeners know just what kind of employer he is. "One rewarding scene was to watch young man who was deeply involved with drugs and alcohol; a physical wreck and not likely to be hired. He wanted a job and Dan gave him a chance. At first it did not work out well. The young man finally realized he needed to change. He became a dependable employee." There would be many with similar problems along the way; and many stories of changed lives.

Dan and Mildred's vision for the retail produce markets, knowledge of their customers buying habits and instinct for what the next retail trend would be is remarkable. They have done it without spreadsheets or marketing polls. They listen and they connect with people. Providing their markets with even more products and produce meant that Dan, who did all the produce buying, with the support of his employees and family, would have to travel to where the local crops were ready for market. Their own grown produce was doing well in their season but they needed produce every week of the year. They retailed about 200 tons of produce each week, a combination of the produce from their own farms and greenhouses and those products they purchased wholesale. Dan would leave home at 2 AM on Tuesday morning and head for the Philadelphia produce market. Here he would purchase what was available and what he needed. There was no one better his employees will say. Dan knew that if you buy right you could make money. They are amazed at his ability to work numbers and remember prices in his head. He could tell what he paid for grapes four weeks ago. He would walk down through the market stopping to taste everything. Deals were made without recording prices. Dan knew exactly what he paid for everything. And he bought a lot of skids of produce. From Philadelphia he flew to Columbia, South Carolina when the crops were at their peak. He would purchase a load of tomatoes and watermelon, cantaloupe and peaches. He flew back to Philadelphia on Wednesday night and stopped back at the produce market to buy whatever else was needed before returning home. And the deals made on Tuesday were honored, even if an item was cheaper on his return trip. Dan will say, "You make your deal and you live by it. Right or wrong. You live by it." His retail theory has always been, "Sell value at the lower prices." Dan was known for treating people fairly when doing business, buying at the lowest price as he possibly could, but always treating people fairly. He was well respected and liked at the Philadelphia Market.

Produce Buying and Trucking Stories

It was on one such produce buying trip to Columbia, South Carolina that Dan spotted a huge load of beautiful quality honeydew melons on an open bed stake body sixty foot trailer. Dan and the owner/driver entered into negotiating a deal. It took a lot of negotiating, Dan recalls but he did get the driver to agree to his price of eight cents each. The price included delivery to the packing house at the Spinnerstown farm. The driver's major concern was that a sixty foot trailer was an illegal vehicle in Pennsylvania but he was anxious to sell and accepted Dan's offer.

The melons were delivered on schedule without any problems. The melons had been field grown in Texas. Picked and loaded from the fields the melons were taken to the Wholesale Produce Market in Columbia, SC. The final destination was to our markets in Pennsylvania, quite a journey. For Dan this remains one of the most challenging purchases he has ever made. And one with exciting results. The load numbered between three and four thousand, Dan recalls, and were sold out that weekend at the four farm markets; Emmaus, Allentown, and the produce stands at the Allentown Fairgrounds and at Zern's in Gilbertsville.

There are bound to be challenges and unusual stories over the years when your business involves hauling fresh produce and live plants. On one occasion a tractor trailer load was sent out from the farm in Spinnerstown to make a delivery just south of Baltimore, Maryland. The delivery was made without any issues. However, on the way home the driver got tired and pulled off to the side of the road. Unaware that the ground was quite saturated from recent rains in the location, the truck got stuck in the mud. The driver chose not to seek any help and hitchhiked home. He just left the truck set there. Needless to say that was the last load the driver hauled for Dan.

Some stories are now comical. Though the exact details are not recalled, Dan tells of a driver with a load of foliage plants on a cold winter day making a return trip from Florida. As was customary the trailer had propane heater tanks to keep the plants from freezing in transit. The driver was traveling on Interstate 95 just south of Baltimore intending to go through the tunnel. As was entering the tunnel he spotted a "No propane tanks allowed" sign. He was already too far into the tunnel to turn around. He backed all the way out. Dan still wonders how the driver managed that without an accident or a police escort or traffic fines.

Deliveries need to be made and they need to be on time. Some trips are challenging for drivers to manipulate through cities. A nearly brand new truck was sent from the farm with a load to Hunts Point Wholesale Produce Market, in Bronx, New York. The driver felt great about being behind the wheel of this new truck. He forgot to check on the height of the truck. He attempted to cross under a low railroad bridge in the city. A lot of damage was done to the top of the new truck. The driver drove the truck back to the farm, stopped by the office to see Dan and dropped the keys on Dan's desk. And the he left. He was sure he was going to be fired. Dan had no intention of firing him, in fact Dan sent him to make another delivery to the same location the very next day. Dan and the driver are now partners in business. The driver is a long time, valued employee who once made an error in judgment and found Dan to be a forgiving employer who valued him and helped him grow and learn the business.

During a very busy Easter flower delivery week a lot of drivers are needed and hired. Sometimes a driver is hired who probably should not have been. It happens. A newly hired driver stopped at a hotel where he hit overhead decking. The driver left the damaged truck and disappeared. At the farm everyone was busy. So busy that no one missed the truck or the driver. Three or four days later the hotel manager called the office to find out what was going on with the truck and the driver. This was the first anyone had even missed that truck or the driver. The matter was solved with the hotel. The driver was never heard from again.

A produce market in Leola, PA emerged in the mid-eighties. Many conservative farmers and others were switching from growing tobacco to growing vegetables. At the startup of the Leola produce auction, there were not enough buyers to keep the prices at fair value to the growers. Dan often purchased a large volume at fair prices for both the buyer and the farmers. He was invited to meetings to show the group how to best pack produce and what kind of containers to use; ones that could be stacked on trucks. The farmers themselves began to a good job of growing and packing their own produce. Today there are produce auctions at eleven locations in Pennsylvania.

A New Chapter

In 1987 Dan was honored with the Mid-Atlantic Master Farmer award in recognition of his outstanding contributions to agriculture. A prestigious award given annually, its honorees are nominated and chosen by peers because they "produce intensely. They

Poinsettias became one of Dan's most successful greenhouse products. In 1986 the gross greenhouse sales reached $3 million.

demonstrate long-term progress, consistent with their resources. They are sharp on business, finances and marketing. Their operations are uncommonly efficient." (Mid-Atlantic Master Farmer Awards Luncheon, March, 1987) This award is a lifetime achievement for Dan as an agribusinessman and produce farmer; one that he has not taken lightly. It is an honor that he continues to represent well. With his family and business partners by his side he was presented the award in March of 1987at a celebration banquet. As he was being introduced, it was said of him that he not only was a Master Farmer he was also a "Master Marketer."

Fifty-three year old Dan would undergo quadruple bypass surgery in 1987. It was time to make major business decisions. "Life is a gift from God and it was time to appreciate it more," Mildred reflects about this time in their journey. After much prayer and consideration the clear choice for Dan and Mildred was to cut back. All three Dan Schantz Farm Markets were sold. Dan was making deals right up to his being anesthetized for surgery, taking one more call in the surgical prep unit to close a deal.

They would no longer grow vegetables. They would focus on their growing greenhouse operation and increase the production of plants, flowers and fall ornamentals. There were 605 wholesale accounts to manage. A job Dan was doing alone. Many of the chain store retail markets orders were at the store level at this time; then there were orders from small local stores, road stands, 7-11 convenience stores. An individual Grants or a Woolworth store manager would call in, Dan wrote up the order and the delivery agreement. Dan was on the phone arranging sales for long hours each day. When he wasn't in the office he was on his phone in his car. He loved the contact with clients and the deal making. He knew he had a product line that would sell at the retail level. And he knew he had production employees he could count on to make delivery of their products. Dan and Mildred saw that the wholesale business is where the company would grow from. With the closing of the stores key longtime employees were offered new positions, including a sales team to learn from Dan and take over some of the accounts.

Retail greenhouse on Lehigh Street lot after sale of Big Barn market.

The unusual deal of the sale of the Big Barn store took place in one day. A location was arranged, the attorneys met and the secretaries prepared papers from early in the morning until ten that night, just a week or two after Dan's bypass surgery.

As part of the deal of the sale of the Big Barn Market to a southern New Jersey car dealer, who purchased the property, a corner lot would be retained and used by Dan for fifteen years. A retail greenhouse and garden center was built.

This successful venture kept the Dan Schantz retail name and market a part of the Lehigh Valley retail greenhouse market. The current retail market built just off of Lehigh Street is a mile away. Dan and Mildred have been a retail markets and greenhouses presence along this stretch of road in the west Allentown area for forty-seven years.

Fall Ornamentals

This was now the time when Dan and Mildred concentrated on the greenhouse operations. They worked to expand their fall ornamental product line, growing approximately seven hundred acres of pumpkins, gourds, Indian corn and squash. The greenhouse production crew is still busy

Dan and Mildred's great grandchildren, Millie and Callen enjoy visiting the Lehigh Street store. Here they are pictured with the annual "great pumpkin."

shipping garden mums when the time to begin harvesting, packing and shipping the fall ornamentals. The picking needs to begin by mid-August to ensure the products are ready for orders. The first orders are most often shipped on or near August twentieth of each year. Fall ornamental production is labor intensive.

The three kinds of Indian corn grown; strawberry, mini-finger and regular are all brought to the packing house area where the husk is pulled back, they are sorted and bunched.

From here the corn is taken to a designated greenhouse area for drying. The area is partitioned off with heavy plastic sheeting, heated and dried, large fans are set up to move the air. The dried ears are ready to ship and will be delivered with little concern for black spots of mold showing. Dan and Mildred consistently take care to send out quality products.

Thousands of gourds mini and cutie pie pumpkins arrive from the fields to be washed, sorted, dried, waxed and dried again. Each is checked to be sure they are good. By conveyor belt they are sent to the boxing area. This all takes place in one complete production line. The larger pumpkins are also washed and sorted in another area of the packing houses. Ones that are the proper size are sorted out to carts for hand painting. The carts used allow for two rows of pumpkins, facing out for easier painting in minimal time. Painted pumpkins are shipped in display boxes on pallets. The fall ornamental product lines have been good business for Dan and Mildred. The total number of trucks loaded and sent out for delivery each day during the busy spring plant season and the fall ornamental season is typically fifteen straight job and twenty-five to thirty 53' trailer loads. It has been estimated that if all the tractor trailers of a season's fall ornamentals were lined up the length would reach from the Spinnerstown farm out to route 663 near the PA Turnpike entrance, a distance of about three and a half miles.

Pumpkins may only be grown on the same field one time in a four year cycle. This has meant finding and renting a lot of fields. In the late eighties the orders needed more fall ornamentals than their field could provide. Dan and Mildred became in contact with a grower in Farmington, New Mexico. They purchased some of his crop and found it to be of good quality. The grower was leasing rich fertile soil on the Navaho Indian Reservation. The land was in 160 acre circles with pivot irrigation.

Telephone contacts assured Dan that this was the place to grow pumpkins and Indian Corn. One advantage they found was that because there was no morning dew the husks on the corn, when dry stayed nearly white. Locally the husks, when dry, often have dark mildew spotting. The grower had assured Dan that there would be plenty of laborers to harvest the crops.

Dan and Mildred had signed up to go on a tour through Texas and Mexico in January of 1989. Dan made arrangements to meet the grower in Brownsville, Texas on the day before the tour began. A partnership was formed and the deal to grow 1325 acres of pumpkins; divided into 1100 acres of large size ones and 225 of small size, 100 acres of Indian corn and 75 acres of gourds on land leased from the Navaho Indians in Farmington, New Mexico. The deal was set and the crops were planted.

Dan and Mildred made a trip to see the crops—they were growing beautifully and on schedule. The area was amazing to see. Mildred described the area as appearing to have mountains all around when viewed from the town. A drive through rough terrain led to the area where there were beautiful 160 acre circles of many different crops each with irrigation. The Indians crops had first water rights.

It was a good crop. The Indian corn husks were nearly white as promised. There were some challenges with harvesting that first year, but not ones that would make Dan and Mildred want to give up on the first try. Similar crops were planted the next year. The promise was that the harvesting would go better. A warehouse was purchased in Farmington where Navaho Indian ladies were hired to assemble fall decorative wreaths using mini Indian corn and calico patches. A very expensive ad was placed in Better Homes and Gardens magazine. There was little interest from the ad and sales were very poor.

The second year's crop was very good. The difficulty was in getting it harvested. The work was too labor intensive. Most of the crop did not get harvested that year.

A large sum of money had been borrowed to finance this venture's crop, warehouse and supplies. Though the deal was meant to be a partnership, Dan was left to repay the entire loan. Needless to say, this was the last year Dan and Mildred would be part of fall ornamental business in New Mexico.

Business Partnership

Dan and Mildred met Jeff Trainer in the eighties. Jeff was a young sales rep for the packaging firm they used as a supplier. Dan saw Jeff's potential and enthusiasm for making deals. They formed a partnership know as DJ Management. Their business partnership is focused on real estate development. They have a keen vision to see in properties what others may not. They take the risk and invest. Jeff shares that Dan has always looked at each deal for its potential to advance the quality of life in the community. It has to be a benefit to the community or it is turned down. Their first investment was to purchase the previously sold 2102 Union Blvd market property and convert the building into a strip mall, leasing space to a number of small stores. They purchased the former Traub Market on Emmaus Avenue in Allentown. The building was renovated, space was added and a strip mall with Valley Farm Market as the anchor store was developed. Some deals were on paper. A mobile home park was bought and sold on the same day. Their investments have included bowling alleys, office buildings, housing and high rise apartments, and condominiums; land for a bank and businesses. They also have included other investors in their deals over the years. They had the plans and the financial backing to build an ice hockey arena in Allentown at the site of the former Hess's Department Store in 2001. The finances and details seemed to be in order to build a 7000 seat ice hockey arena. With a lot of effort they were granted a tax-free zone for the project. The project fell through when the Industrial development authority made plans for PPL to take over this area to build a utilities trading center.

They purchased land to develop the Steel Ice rink in South Bethlehem in 2003 This community ice skating facility and hockey training center with regulation size rinks continues to thrive in the heart of the developing ArtsQuest SteelStack art and culture center of South Bethlehem. Jeff Parks then the CEO of ArtsQuest affirms Dan's vision for community, "For so many years, Dan Schantz Greenhouses donated the lovely flowers for the beautiful gardens at Musikfest's Blumenplatz

venue. Today, their plants and
flowers add a special and very
colorful element to Musikfest,
Christkindlmarkt Bethlehem
and Oktoberfest as well as the
Banana Factory and SteelStacks.
On behalf of everyone in the
community, we thank Dan,
Mildred and the entire Schantz

family for all of their support over the years. Their support of ArtsQuest
and our events demonstrates their commitment to the community while
helping create a very memorable experience for so many people over the
decades."

New Retail Locations

Dan Schantz Greenhouse and Cut Flower Outlet opened in 2002.
This new retail location would be one in which the vision for a cut flower
market became a reality. The arrangements are made in the store by
professional staff and the fresh flowers are ready for purchase. The cut
flower staff, under the management of Connie Schantz, provides floral
services for customers. Weddings, funerals, family events, recitals and
proms and any occasion can be accommodated. Their arrangements are
lush and beautiful. They have taken many a brides vision for her day
come to reality through their creativity and vision.

In 2005 a second retail location was opened in west Bethlehem.
Both locations had spacious greenhouses for seasonal plants and bedding
flowers, vegetables, indoor plants and foliage, gifts and home gardening
supplies. Dan keeps a close eye on the retail markets. He checks on
signage and displays to ensure they are ready for the weekly ad features.

The retail location on Lehigh Street, Allentown, PA

Dan and Mildred Schantz

Left: Mildred Schantz checking plants and display details.

Dan Schantz Cut Flower and Greenhouses retail market on Lehigh Street includes cut flowers, arrangements and full floral services, garden giftware, bedding plants, annuals, perennials, foliage, seeds, bulbs, garden supplies, shrubbery, seeds and bulbs, and much more.

The Lehigh Shopping Center store closing in 2011.

On any given week he will project to the store manager what the sales figures will be. He is most often correct. The staff knows he will be in the store on a Wednesday to do his weekly walk through. They learn retail wisdom from both Dan and Mildred. Labels are facing out toward the customers view; yellow mums are not to be displayed next to white mums. The details in displays sell the products and the displays need to be neat and clean. "If you have time to lean, you have time to clean" "You must clean up the corners to make money." And if an empty spot is noted, they will hear Dan again quip, "Are we trying to sell empty space?" And as he leaves the store, they hear Dan say, "Carry on."

The Bethlehem store was closed in 2011. The staff found it difficult to do so. Dan kept them all encouraged through the process. They had a strong loyal customer base that came to the store and cried and brought cookies to the closing. The former staff still gets together once a month for breakfast.

Awards

D an Schantz Farm and Greenhouses LLC has received awards from the industry and from national businesses who have recognized them for their quality products and work as vendors. They continue to rank in the top 100 growers nationwide. The business community and professional associations have recognized and honored Dan for his contributions to leadership and service.

He was an active member of the Pennsylvania Vegetable Growers Association (PVGA) for more than 40 years. He was president of the association three times during those years. He also actively served on committees, notably the Convention committee. Under his leadership, there was an expansion of the educational sessions and speakers in an effort to advance the educational value of the Conference to the growers. The PVGA honored Dan with a Life Membership in the Association in 2005 at the Fruit and Vegetable Growers Dinner. The family and business partners surprised Dan by also being present at the dinner. Dan spotted Tommy in a doorway at the banquet. He was thrilled to have them there with him and Mildred. Dan received the award for "his extraordinary leadership, vision, dedication, and support he has freely given to the Association and the vegetable industry in Pennsylvania." (PA Vegetable Growers News, February, 2005) Appointed in 1988 by the Secretary of Agriculture from nominations submitted by growers, Dan served on the Board of the Pennsylvania Marketing and Research Program for twenty years. When he resigned in 2008 he was the only board member still remaining of the original group. This Board seeks to serve vegetable growers through promotion and funding of vegetable production research.

The Journey Continues

It is the next season for the greenhouses at the Spinnerstown farm. For those doing the planning, it is already the next year. It is a journey of many steps to grow the beautiful products sent out each season from the greenhouses. Dan and Mildred have now entrusted their employees with the task. The employees seek to keep the same signature quality and value for each product. It is what Dan and Mildred want for the business they grew from the seeds of their faith.

So I decided there is nothing better than to enjoy food and drink and to find satisfaction in work. Then I realized that these pleasures are from the hand of God. Ecclesiastes 2:2 NLT

For Christmas in 1984, Dan and Mildred were presented with this framed poster by their employees. Designed and drawn by Barbara Schoenk, an office employee who worked in advertising and artwork as well as serving as the editor of the staff newsletter. The poster is hung in Dan and Mildred's Quakertown Home.

Employees: The Family of Business

"He has been a second father to me," is often the declared by the employees of Dan Schantz as they thoughtfully reflect on their relationship with Dan. On first meeting, he was intimidating to many. He wanted things done right. He needed them done on time. Dan worked hard his entire life and has the same expectation for each of his employees.

Dan and Mildred have held their employees close. From the first day on the job. While Dan and Mildred have high expectations for performance from each of their employees, they have also worked tirelessly beside them to show them what they wanted done. And at times they have patiently shown them again and again just how to do a task. They have supported personal and professional achievement in each employee. They want them each to be the best they can be, in their work and in their personal lives. This has been demonstrated by Dan's open office door and Mildred's presence, patience and encouraging words. The support is practical, simple and kind. They generously have offered assistance and have always offered forgiveness. In their business there is a daily demonstration of Christian character. If there are emotions to express, Dan will express them. But as many employees have testified, they never heard Dan swear. A statement they wished could be said of themselves.

It is no wonder then that for many employees this is the only job they have ever held. Whenever a valued employee has decided that he or she needed a change in employment, Dan would always encourage them to go. He would also tell them that if it did not work out, they would be welcomed back.

A family work place is also perfect environment for love to blossom. Over the years a number of Dan and Mildred's employees have found their true love while both were working at the markets or in the greenhouses. Dan and Mildred smile when they share this tidbit. And after all, their marriage is a wonderful model of a loving marriage and strong partnership.

Back Row: Nevin Davis, John Carl, Stephen Thomas, Paul Hardiman, Cynthia Eckenrode
Front Row: Lisa Myers, Dennis Heilman, Patrick Flanley, Daniel Schantz
2002 photo taken at the Grand Opening of Lehigh Street retail store, Dan Schantz
Greenhouse and Cut Flower Outlet.

Dan Schantz Farm and Green House, LLC today is a partnership of eight long time employees of Dan and Mildred Schantz. Trusted with the Dan Schantz product they work diligently to continue to promote the sense that this is a family company. They take pride in what each one contributes to provide every customer with their quality product.

Dan took Patrick Flanley on as his partner in 1992. Dan, his son Tommy and Patrick shared the partnership; Dan held the majority shares. Patrick took the title of General Manager. His work involved every aspect of the greenhouse operations and the fall field crops.

In 2001, Tommy decided to sell his shares in the company to pursue other interests in the development properties Dan held. Dan and Mildred offered several long time employees the opportunity to purchase a percentage of ownership shares. Eight employees and Dan and Mildred formed the LLC partnership in 2002. Each partner brings their unique gifts and leadership abilities to the business. Together they keep the name and the vision of Dan and Mildred on each product and through each season.

In 2012, Dan and Mildred sold their remaining shares to Patrick. Patrick now holds the majority shares of Dan Schantz Farm and

Greenhouses LLC. Dan continues to be a vital part of the business. Dan goes to the office as an employee now. He gives oversight to the retail operations and is there to offer input and wisdom. He weekly meets with the retail staff and does a store walk-through. Here he checks displays; are there enough arrangements in the fresh flower cases, including the dozen rose's arrangements? Are the weekly feature items easily found and tagged accurately? Every detail is noticed. He is relied on and respected as the expert. Dan will often take a call from an employee who needs to know pricing of a product, and without looking it up, Dan can quote the price from several years and will set a price based on today's market. It is his gift.

The Partners (in alphabetical order)

John Carl became a partner in Dan Schantz Farm and Greenhouse in 2002.

John Carl was just thirteen years old when he came to the farm to pick strawberries. He helped out part time as a teenager on the farm and later at the market stands. After graduating from High School he became a full time employee. How did he learn the produce business? How did Dan and Mildred ensure that their business' signature display style was carried out by John and his coworkers? They showed them. They worked alongside of them. First you learned how to set up to do a task, and then you learned the task. If it was apples to be displayed in baskets, the first row was as important as the last row. And they showed them how to do it exactly. And they showed them again. And they showed them again. John recalls that, "Each task and display was done exceptionally, or you started over again. Nothing was thrown together." John also remembers the hours spent on Thursday nights to get ready for the weekend specials at the markets. Everything was done right and well. This was what Dan and Mildred wanted for their customers, their best efforts. For John it was hard work but it was enjoyable throughout his employment; in each position.

After he graduated from High School his work at Dan Schantz Farms became his fulltime employment. He spent his days going to markets and learning the retail produce trade. In 1978, John was transferred to the new Lehigh Street Big Barn store. It was at this store he was promoted to manager. John remained at the store as manager until it as well as the other farm markets was sold.

THE KING $39.99

THE DUKE $16.99

THE PRINCE $10.99

THE MARQUIS $8.99   THE DUCHESS $12.99   THE PRINCESS $18.99   THE QUEEN $23.99

Fruit baskets had been a part of the product line for some time. Sold year round, but most popular at Christmas, Easter and Mother's Day the baskets ranged in size from small to bushel basket size. This item was most popular at Christmas when several thousand were made up and sold in the markets. The sale of the all three markets in 1987, brought the idea of a market specializing in Fresh Fruit Baskets. The idea was developed into a business. John was a partner in this venture along with Dan, Jeff Trainer and Brad DeHoff. John was the manager of the fruit basket shop, Nature's Nectar, when it opened at 4th and Susquehanna Streets in Allentown.

The closing of this shop marked the end of an era. They were now completely out of the produce business. Growing plant and flower greenhouse business became the focus of the business. The only field crops grown are fall ornamentals.

John was transferred from the closed Lehigh Street market to the Sales Department at the Main Office at the Spinnerstown farm. He learned the marketing of a product by working beside Dan. He learned to work on the road, moving their product and finding new customers. Dan would set a goal for the week and John and others would be on the phone making deals until the dollar amount was reached. It was all done by phone contact personal conversations. This was a time long before an email or a text message was customer contact.

Dan and he made a trip to Boston together to call on a chain store as a potential customer. Upon arrival at the chain store office, Jack Wilson, of Stop 'n Shop markets, told them, "Don't sit down, you won't be here long." They did not make a sale. John continued to make phone calls to them. Could they supply them a current product from this seasons' line? John did not give up on Jack Wilson becoming a potential customer. Then late one Saturday a phone call came from Jack. He wanted a product and it had to be delivered the next day. There was talk that it could not be done. It was done. That was the kind of service Dan Schantz provides his wholesale and retail customers. The relationship that came about from the personal contact and persistence developed into a loyal long-term partnership with Jack and Stop & Shop, which is now an Ahold USA market and was integrated into Stop &Shop/Giant-Landover.

Today, John's Sales Manager work involves the management of the large chain store accounts and individual accounts. Dan says you cannot name a grocery store chain on the east coast that does not have an account with Dan Schantz Farm and Greenhouses. One of his major accounts is Lowes, serving forty-seven locations from PA through the New England coast. John still keeps his contacts personal and travels to Lowes Headquarters in Morrisville, NC two to four times a year to meet with buyers. Much of the contact work is done through email. John still values making the phone call to personally promote the products and the work that many employees have done to provide them with the Dan Schantz Farm and Greenhouses quality. He continues to emphasis that they remain a family company. Forty-four years in the employment of Dan Schantz Farm and Greenhouse John became a partner in 2002. Working for Dan and Mildred is the only paying job John has ever had.

Nevin Davis became a partner in Dan Schantz Farm and Greenhouse in 2002.

Nevin Davis grew up at the Spinnerstown farm. His parents, Gene and Elsie began working on the farm when Nevin was eleven years old. Nevin started mowing the lawn for Dan and Mildred when he was thirteen. When he was old enough, he worked on the farm and at markets. He recalls that there was "no sitting still, Mildred always had something for you to do." Yet he loved the work. Mildred made it fun and would often kid around as you worked at setting up for Market. Nevin left to do other employment for five years. He returned and has remained a valuable employee. He drove truck for the business making runs to Florida for watermelon and delivering products up and down the Eastern Coast. Nevin will say that Dan is very forgiving. It took one experience making a delivery in a new truck to show him just how forgiving. Nevin drove to Hunts Point, a New York City neighborhood, and got lost. He struck an el overpass and ripped the top off of the truck. Nevin came back to the office and tossed the truck keys on Dan's desk, certain that he would be fired. And he was very regretful of that happening. Dan did not fire him. Yes, Nevin speaks of Dan's forgiving character with a thankful heart.

Today Nevin is in charge of purchasing perennials, shrubbery and Christmas Trees for the retail markets. Nevin travels to farms and suppliers in North Carolina and throughout Pennsylvania to purchase Christmas trees. Of the five to six thousand trees purchased, most of them are the now popular Frasier fir tree. They will retail at least five other variety of trees along with fresh greens and wreaths. Nevin can often be found offloading and setting up trees at the Lehigh Street store in December. Shrubbery and perennials are purchased by Nevin for spring sales beginning in February. He works second shift during the spring and fall busy shipping season. After the trucks return from their daily deliveries it is his job to be sure that the team gets right order on the right truck for the deliveries the next day. This can mean that loads for up to 45 trucks are filled at night during spring shipping and 25 to thirty loads each day during the fall shipping season. Additionally, he keeps the greenhouse equipment in working condition and also works on inventory control. He has been employed for thirty-seven years with Dan and Mildred.

C ynthia Eckenrode became a partner in Dan Schantz Farm and Greenhouse in 2002.

Cynthia was originally hired as a grower in the greenhouses. She began working for Dan in 1984 right after graduation from Penn State University where she earned a Bachelor of Science degree in Horticulture. She is now the Greenhouse Manager of the Spinnerstown Greenhouses. She a lot of her work is done at a computer. Travel is a vital part of the job for Cindy.

Her travels take her to Walmart headquarters in Bentonville, AK and to the Lowes headquarters in Mooresville, NC. The meetings with company representatives are about plants and planters. She makes sure that the orders for the next season are exactly as they want them to be. She plans and designs combinations of plants to be used in container pots and hanging baskets. Next step for Cindy is ordering containers, both pots and hanging baskets. The plants she orders arrive in to the greenhouses as rooted and unrooted cuttings. And finally a critical stage of getting the containers right for the orders is being sure that the right PUC sticker is on each pot, pack or hanging basket. This is just one aspect of her many and varied duties.

Cindy is a member of the Nationwide New Variety Council. She along with five or six other growers will meet to review and choose which varieties, some new and some old, will be featured the following year. The group meets six to seven times a year in Bentonville, AK. Cindy travels to California and at times to Europe, where she is looking to find what potentially can be the next new plant and flower varieties for the business. By traveling to trial gardens held by seed companies, attending garden expos and meetings about the latest varieties and equipment Cindy knows the best products to add to greenhouse offerings.

Cindy also serves on the Lowes Growers Council. A nationwide committee of six members, they meet several times a year to decide what will be the best to grow and sell at all the Lowes' stores. Presently they are working on the 2016 spring season.

Cindy is a member of the PA Horticulture society. She also serves on the Integrated Marketing Group who seek to improve the chain of varieties and cuttings from various places around the world.

Cindy has been employed for 30 years with Dan and Mildred.

Patrick Flanley became a partner in Dan Schantz Farm in 1992.

Denny Heilman, as manager of the Union Blvd Farm Market, hired teenager Patrick Flanley in 1975. Patrick was hired on the spot. Those first years he worked stocking shelves and unloading trucks. Patrick chuckles when he recalls the early morning Wednesday phone calls from Denny. He would call him up to have him work before school, from 5:30 AM until 7:20. He would go to school and then come back after school. Patrick worked a lot of hours in High School, even on an occasional "sick" day when he was needed. Patrick, though young, showed a keen interest in retail and had the work ethic skills to prove his value as an employee.

After High School graduation he chose to stay on as a fulltime employee at Dan Schantz rather than attend college or work for the railroad as others in his family had. He soon would be promoted to Assistant Manager. As Dan's market business grew so did Patrick's responsibilities. When the new market opened on Easton Avenue in Bethlehem, Patrick was named manager and served there until it was sold in 1987. Patrick helped with the store design and did construction work on the store before its opening. Dan would do a weekly store visit and find everything perfect and tell Patrick and the staff what a good job they had done. Dan would leave and within minutes Patrick would be paged for a phone call. Dan would say, "Pat, don't you want to sweep in the front of your store?" Or "You know there are leaves in the vestibule." It was a rare week that he did not find something. These visits and the calls kept Patrick on his toes as manager and aware of the importance of the details in a stores appearance. Patrick knew Dan was always on the phone. He even had one in his car. Long before anybody had phones Dan had a rotary one; he would tuck it under his chin and drive up the Sckuykill Express way quickly weaving in and out of traffic and making deals and giving orders to the farm office. Yes, Patrick recalls many driving experiences with Dan. One time Dan even asked a State Police Officer when the last time he had his radar checked.

When the store locations closed Patrick transferred to the Main office in Spinnerstown. He did a little bit of everything. He was given sales work to do and hated it. He didn't mind the working with the chain stores but hated the cold calls. He was happy that Denny took over all the sales responsibilities. Patrick spent more time outside instead of in the office. He did a lot of labor working with the help unloading trucks, supervising loading and pulling items from the greenhouses. Dan put him in charge of the operation. He became General Manager of the greenhouses. In 1990 Dan and Mildred moved to their home in Quakertown. Patrick and his wife Karen and their daughters moved into the farmhouse at the Spinnerstown farm. This was quite a relief for Dan, Pat was now in charge of all the dreaded night time greenhouse alarms from power failures or heater problems. His position of General Manager has kept him busy overseeing every aspect of the greenhouses and over the field crops

Patrick became a business partner with Dan in 1992. He was then 24% partner. The partnership grew in 2002 and other longtime employees were added. In August of 2012 Patrick purchased the remained shares owned by Dan and became the majority partner/owner of Dan Schantz Farm and Greenhouses, LLC. This has been Patrick's only job; a lifelong journey through the retail market business to the complexities of the greenhouse business.

Paul Hardiman became a partner in Dan Schantz Farm and Greenhouse in 2002.

Paul Hardiman grew up in Oxford, England. He immigrated to the United States in 1990 and has been working for Dan ever since. His work in the greenhouses began as a section grower. Within a few years he was promoted to the position of Head Grower. Twenty-four years later he continues to be the Head Grower.

His job in simple terms is to oversee all crops in all four greenhouse locations. He and the greenhouse staff check and report on the growth, quality and timing of each crop. It is his job to see that each crop is on schedule and ready to be shipped to the customers on time. This requires the oversight of as many as 25 greenhouse personnel; section growers and those whose main job is to do the watering of the plants. He and his staff take time to look beyond just the "pretty stuff" and look for what does not look right and address any issues. He recommends what spray or chemicals need to be applied at the proper time. He visits each of the four greenhouse locations each week. He takes a personal look at the crops. He adjusts the temperature and checks the root systems. He is charge of making sure the products are in prime condition for the date of delivery with just the right bloom. He needs to be sure they will all finish in top quality. There is no "number two crop" in today's market. Everything is shipped to the required customer specs of their orders or it will be rejected by them.

Dennis Heilman became a partner in Dan Schantz Farm and Greenhouse in 2002.

A boy from the neighborhood, Dennis was twelve the summer of 1967 when he rode his bike up to the farm looking for work. He did odd jobs around the farm that summer, never imagining that it would be the start of lifelong career. Denny is thankful for the second family he found in Dan and Mildred. He received many opportunities and help financially, emotionally and spiritually. And he received what he describes as the "gift of a work ethic." He learned that you had to work hard to survive in this business. Dan's expectations were always high for this young employee, but Dan was always fair and always around to help. From Dan, Denny would learn the right and wrong way to do business. He was taught "how to buy and sell in a respectful manner, taking what was ours, but not taking advantage of someone." From Mildred he learned how to work. As a young man he worked alongside Mildred in the evenings when the laborers were not around. From her he was taught, "First, you get ready to work, then you work." One of his first jobs with her was packing Easter mums after school. He remembers that "she ran me ragged, but I learned the importance of doing the job right and working until the task was done."

Denny can visualize those days that he worked with Dan at the farm market stands. The produce was set up perfect or you did it again.

And customers were not allowed to touch the fruit. There would be Dan, "hollering, bagging and taking money as fast as he could." They stayed until the produce was sold out. Through High School and after graduation Denny continued working for Dan with the exception of three years in the early 80's. He did everything. He drove truck to pick up produce Dan had bought at the Philadelphia Food Center or loads of melons from Laurel Delaware and Cordele Georgia. He worked setting up the Lehigh Street store. Denny worked with his Dad on the Union Boulevard Store from the first day of renovations. He then was given the job of manager of the store. He still recalls a regular customer at the store whom they suspected was shoplifting. They kept a watch on her store visits and finally caught her. The police were called and Denny still cannot believe that when she dumped out her purse there was a wad of cash. She had shoplifted three pounds of bananas. The bananas were selling for twenty cents a pound back then. And they were often on sale for nineteen cents a pound. Denny served as "General Contractor of the Big Barn store on Lehigh Street and then became store manager. When the retail markets were sold Denny transferred to the Main office at the Spinnerstown farm and became a sales manager. He quickly learned to make sales calls and establish customers and become their supply vendor, including Walmart. He continues to manage the Walmart account making trips to Bentonville, Arkansas to meet with the main buyers. Dan Schantz Farm and Greenhouses has been Walmart, "Vendor of the Year" twice. Denny is a partner in Dan Schantz Farm and Greenhouses and is Head of the Sales Department.

L isa Myers became a partner in Dan Schantz Farm and Greenhouse in 2002.

Lisa Myers has been known as "Dan's right arm," as executive assistant and as office manager she has worked closely with Dan for the past twenty years. As the Comptroller of the business Lisa manages all aspects of the company's financial department, including all records, accounting, bookkeeping, insurances payroll and administrative tasks. She gives oversight to those who work in the business office. Lisa is an expert in computer programs used by the business. She works with the office staff and greenhouse personnel in the use of computer software for ordering and inventory.

"If you have a question—ask Lisa," Mildred will say.

Lisa began working for Dan and Mildred in September of 1993. She answered a newspaper ad for a position that had a heading that caught her attention: BEST PERSON. She applied for the position of Office Manager. Nervous at her first interview with Dan she recalls that Saturday morning. Dan quickly reassured her that having a formal education was not necessary for the position. After round-robin interview with several key people, she was chosen for the position from the three candidates. Lisa will say, "my destiny was confirmed." Six months later Lisa left to live with her parents who were moving to North Carolina. She felt she needed to do so as a young widow mom with two young sons . She knew she had disappointed Dan, but he took it in stride and a her replacement was hired. When she was leaving Lisa asked Tommy if he was going to say goodbye. Tommy was quick to reply, "Why? You'll be back. They all come back." By August of 1994 Lisa got a phone call from Dan. He needed her back. Would she think about it? She did and headed back to Pennsylvania. Dan sent two loaders in a straight truck down to North Carolina to pack up her belongings and move her back. She moved into a mobile home on the farm property and was back in the office to work on September 15, 1994. Tommy was right.

Lisa has known and given honor to the Lord for leading her to her job. She is thankful to have had Dan and Mildred readiness to listen and their willingness to care for her, advise her and pray with her. Dan has been more than just a boss; he is a very special man. One whom she can attribute the verse in Micah 6:8 to, "love justice and walk humbly with your God." She has learned a lot about commitment, faith, family, humbleness honesty integrity and generosity from Dan and Mildred through her years of employment. They have taught her through the way they live their lives and how they treat those around them.

Like many others Lisa has been amazed at the kind of gracious hosts Dan and Mildred always have been. Here she has learned and been groomed to be a better hostess. They are always concerned about their guests. She enjoyed being their guest during the years when Dan and Mildred would take the "secretaries to spend the day in New York City. The day began with breakfast; there was time for shopping, Broadway show matinee and then dinner in the Big Apple. Dinner was always at one of the top restaurants in New York City, either Tavern on the Green or The View, the revolving spot atop the Marriott Marquis.

Lisa hesitated to sign a five year employment contract that was a requirement of those signing to come into the partnership. She did not know where she may the Lord may be leading her and her young sons. Dan did not hesitate to add a clause to her contract that allowed her to leave if she needed to do so. To him it was simple; to Lisa it was a dilemma. Dan again showed her how he valued her and how he knew her commitment was not taken lightly. The years have gone by and Lisa has been an employee for twenty years.

S tephen Thomas became a partner in Dan Schantz Farm and Greenhouse in 2002.

Stephen Thomas is an experienced grower and greenhouse facilities manager who was hired 22 years ago. He is originally from Tennessee. He came to the farm with experience from his work in Virginia. Steve is the Superintendent of Greenhouse Operations. He is the person in charge of planning what, when and where to grow each crop. This work involves ordering seeds and then giving direction as to at which of the four greenhouse facilities the seeds are to be grown in and when each variety is to be seeded.

Steve checks temperatures at locations throughout the greenhouse to make sure of proper temperature for each crop. Adjustments are made. Much of this work is done through the use of the Argus system, the computer software and hardware environmental control system for the greenhouses. One of his least favorite duties is to track down and find the problem when the greenhouse alarms go off in the middle of the night due to heating system failure.

Every employee has a part to play in the production of each season's crops. Timing is critical. Orders need to be received early. Next year's orders are in place soon after the end of the current year. Orders are placed from suppliers around the world.

Steve talked about receiving weekly notes from Mildred. He misses her input. It was valued as a part of the big picture of the greenhouse crops that his work entails. There are details, ordering, environmental controls, inventory locations to juggle, but Mildred's eyes saw and she wrote notes on what was going on at the greenhouse floor level. She never missed a detail in her walk-throughs.

Twice each year a seasonal all day wrap-up meeting is held. Thirty to theirty-five people who are in the Sales Department, who are Department Managers, Growers and the Owners would meet for the day.

The spring and summer season meeting is held in July and the Fall and Christmas season meeting is held in February.

Varieties grown are reviewed; areas of the work that were good are discussed as well as what needs to be improved. Plans are made for the next season.

It is also a pep talk meeting. It gives the leadership from all four locations a chance to get recharged for the next season.

Dan Schantz Farm and Greenhouses Long Time Employees		
Employee Name	**Years of Service**	**Department**
Daniel W. Schantz	58	Office
Dennis Heilman	47	Sales
John C. Carl	44	Sales
Joyce Heilman	45	Office
Patrick Flanley	39	Production
Nevein Davis	37	Shipping
Juan A Rivera	36	Production
David Doescher	32	Shipping
Amelio Gonzalez Jr	30	Production
Cynthia Eckenrode	30	Production
Thomas Zale	30	Grower
Raymond Smith Sr	29	Production
Larry Geissinger	27	Grower
Christine Heilman	26	Retail Sales
Connie Schantz	25	Retail Floral
Paul Hardiman	23	Grower
Kevin Hench	23	Production
Stephen Thomas	22	Grower
Lisa Myers	21	Office
Thomas Kehoe	20	Shipping
Ronald Kunkle	20	Driver
Cynthia Thomas	20	Advertising
Susan Masters	19	Retail Sales
Walter Pereau	18	Grower
Elias Botros	17	Grower
Mark Ringenary	17	Production

Dan Schantz Farm and Greenhouses Long Time Employees		
Employee Name	**Years of Service**	**Department**
Ricardo Chacon	16	Production
Ghassan Ferkh	16	Grower
Scott Crothers	16	Driver
Nabil Mamari	15	Grower
Sharon Hyndman	15	Sales
Howaida Elias	15	Retail Sales
Fadi Khouri	14	Grower
Donna Solarek	14	Retail Sales
Jerry Smith	14	Grower
Ken Shao	13	Production
Darlene Brensinger	13	Production
George Shetah	13	Grower
Ramez Boutrous	12	Grower
George Bortz	12	Driver
Kevin Echevarria	12	Production
Lauren Flanley	12	Retail Sales
Brenda Szukics	12	Retail Sales
Felipe Argueta	12	Production
Amanda Trach	11	Production
Dennis McElroy	11	Grower
Bonita Wernett	11	Retail Sales
Sally Hendricks	11	Retail Sales
Juan Gatica	10	Production
Carol Hamscher	10	Retail Sales
Melody Davis	over 10	Retail Sales

Chart of 2012 Plant and Vegetables Products

Product	Grown for Wholesale & Retail	Supplied Wholesale	Supplied for Retail Market
Poinsettia (Over 30 varieties)	1,000,000 +		
Christmas Trees			5,000
Greens/Wreaths/Cemetery Logs			4.600+
Garden Mums (Hardy)	1,000,000 +		
Character Mums	420,000		
Pumpkins/Gourds All Fall items	429 Tracker Trailer loads (670 acres)		
2012 Big Pumpkin for Retail store Purchased each year			827.5 lbs. (2012) Largest ever was - 1475 lbs.
Painted/Printed Pumpkins		540,000	
Indian Corn	250,000 (75 acres)		
Mini Corn/ Strawberry Corn	54,100 (14 acres)		
Straw Bales/Designer Bales		3,900	
Bulbs from Netherlands	3,772,950 (total)		
Crocus	124,000		
Daffodil	120,950		
Tete a Tete (Narcissus)	427,650		
Muscari (Grape Hyacinth)	60,750		
Hyacinth	563,800		
Tulip	2,095,800		
White Lily	280,000		
Colored Lilies	100,000		
Hanging Baskets	824,825		
Pansies (plants)	1,000,000		
Annuals from seed	22,600,000		
Vegetables	900,000		
Proven Winners		67,000	
Herbs		128,000	
Planters, combination All sizes		133,000	
Tropical Foliage Plants (Includes succulents)		267,000	
Accent Plants		539,000	
Deluxe Quart Flowers		660,000	
Geraniums All sizes		743,500	
Wave Petunias		1,067,000	
Assorted Flowers Including 300 + varieties of perennials		2,200,022	
Landscaping Shrubs (27 varieties)			As need demands
Cut Roses - Retail only			110,000

DAN SCHANTZ GREENHOUSE

Plants and Flowers for Every Season

The Greenhouse Growing Cycle

This week's advertisement, a full page spread in the Morning Call, will feature items from the farm's current product line, the seeds or cuttings of which were planted up to six months earlier. Designed for year round production, the greenhouses cycle through each year with very little down time. The story can be told by the monthly calendar, but growing things have their own timing, their own seasons. To have the best product available to the public in full bloom and at their peak requires that careful planning and timing takes place. Dan and Mildred set the beginning of this cycle into place nearly sixty years ago. While products and varieties change, the cycle remains the same.

January begins a new calendar year. Stores, homes, churches and businesses are still enjoying their Christmas poinsettias. Just weeks ago the same greenhouses that were lush vibrant acres of poinsettia are now barren with little or no evidence of there having been such a display. Each new season pushes out the last. The empty greenhouse is cleared, swept, scrubbed and sanitized. It is time to move into the next phase of Easter flower and bedding plants production. Easter Sunday, a date that can range between late

The refridgerated bulb cooler rooms house 3-4 million bulbs each fall for spring sales. Photo above shows a hyacinth ready to be packed and shipped to wholesale accounts.

March and late April, is a critical target date that requires an adjustment in production scheduling each year.

Over three million hyacinth, tulip, daffodil and crocus bulbs planted and cooled in large refrigeration units before Thanksgiving. They are moved into greenhouse floors to promote and nurture further growth.

Daylight, shading, temperature, feeding and watering are all carefully recorded and adjusted to ensure full growth rate and bloom in time for shipping contracts with vendors.

Lilies, a flower featured for Easter Sunday are potted and placed into greenhouses. The timing of the shipping of these plants, with their blooms still tight needs to be perfect. Their blooms must open at the retail sale site for the date of this year's Easter Sunday.

Six transplanting lines at Zionsville location. On the two lines using automatic planters, 400 to 700 flats per hour can be transplanted on each line depending on variety and container size.

Seeding and transplanting of spring bedding flowers begins in November and continues through early May. Pansies and other varieties of cold weather bedding plants as well as cold crop veggies are sown in early February and need to be ready to ship in mid-April. Each variety specific rate of growth is carefully calculated and adjusted. This is the science of horticulture. Tiny cuttings under a half inch in size from Central America, Israel, Chili and South Africa are planted in December through April and are ready for the production line transplanting into hanging baskets and large pots. Designs for the combination of varieties in planters are the work of the Dan Schantz personnel. Big box stores also place orders of specific plant groupings and pot design. The automated planting system keeps a daily production staff of up to 730 (2014) busy. The challenge for the staff at the farm is to grow every item so it is ready to ship for display and purchase at their peak bloom.

Mother's Day production focuses on the final preparations of hanging baskets, container gardens and potted annuals. Bedding plants, herbs and perennials for the home gardener are shipped through July 4th and are available at retail locations through August. Every staff member is busy. Everyone is working long hours to get the best of the product line to the customers.

As the bedding plant season slows down, the greenhouses are cleaned, disinfected and prepped for mid-May and early June planting of hardy garden mums from cuttings.

Mums are also grown outdoors on twenty-five acres of fields as well as in shaded greenhouses to push a bloom by mid- July. The first of the hardy mums are ready to be shipped in mid-July. Shipping continues through October.

Character mums are a feature product through Fall, Winter and Spring Holidays. White pom-pom mums are grown and transformed into Turkeys, Santas, Leprechauns and Bunnies. The transformation is all by hand. The features and a bit of sparkle are carefully added to each bloom. These have been an exclusive product design since the first ones were crafted in the mid-90's.

Seven hundred and fifty acres of pumpkins and gourds and ornamental corn are planted in mid to late May. By the beginning of September the fall ornamentals have taken over the much of the greenhouse production focus.

Production lines of ornamental corn is shucked, dried and packed.

Pumpkins and gourds are harvested shipped to the packing houses where they are washed and packaged. Gourds are washed and polished with edible wax prior to shipping.

Each year over one half million gourds and pumpkins are pad printed or hand-painted.

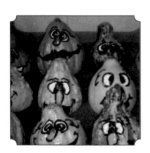

Poinsettia planted in mid – May through early August push the last of the fall plants and ornamentals out of the greenhouses. Full production for over one million poinsettias is underway. Roots are spot checked daily to monitor watering. These temperature sensitive plants require special handling and natural light to ensure they are in full color for the Christmas season.

The seasons have changed. The year-end wrap up meetings and reports are done and another year is already six months in production.

Pictured poinsettia left inset: in mid-October; bottom right: plants in early September; and the vibrant color of the poinsettia ready to be sold by November 10.

Poinsettia Trees. Since the 2010 opening of the Sands Casino in Bethlehem, Dan Schantz Farm and Greenhouses, LLC has bid to place and care for the poinsettia holiday trees display in the casino entrance. The frames for the three trees are two ten foot and one fifteen foot in height. The ten foot frame holds 175 six inch pots and the fifteen foot frame hold 385 six inch pots. The plants are placed into the frames just before Thanksgiving. Plants are watered and replaced as needed by a Dan Schantz employee.

Different varieties are used from year to year; sometimes plants that have been sprinkled with glitter are used, other times some white poinsettia are placed among the red ones.

The poinsettia trees are on display from Thanksgiving until after New Year's Day.

Dan Schantz Farm & Greenhouses, LLC
Locations

8025 Spinnerstown Road, Zionsville, PA

This is the location of the original farm and first greenhouse on the property purchased by Dan and Mildred in 1957. It is now 995,795 square feet (23 acres) of greenhouses, offices and buildings.

1133 Ebenezer Church Road, Rising Sun, MD

This location was first leased in 2008. The greenhouses and shipping buildings are 430,000 square feet (10 acres.)

Dan Schantz Farm & Greenhouses, LLC
Locations

6071 Durham Road, Pipersville, PA

Purchased in 2010, This location includes greenhouses, shipping buildings and offices are 503,989 square feet (11.5 acres). The property includes a home and 60 acres of land.

2671 Old Bethlehem Pike, Quakertown, PA

The property is 153, 216 square feet (3.5 acres.)

Part Three

*"I thank my God in all my
remembrance of you."*
Philippians 1:3

Dan's Reminiscing

" *L* ooking back I see things now that I would do differently. All in all my life, back to my early years of farming during my High School days, I was always busy working and thinking about my next project. Married at the age of nineteen, living in the Koon's apartment for three and a half years we were anxious to buy our own farm. In 1957 we purchased the ninety-six acre farm in Lower Milford Township, Pennsylvania.

Now we could get serious about what we were going to do.

Growing and retailing produce was always in my blood. Finding just how to go about making a living from it was a learning experience and adventure.

At first I tried retailing produce in a huckster route in East Allentown. After two years I found that this was not to be the way I wanted to go. I sold that business. I soon found that road stands and farm markets had much more potential and proved to be a source of opportunities and endless challenges. Between farming fields and our weekend markets I also learned the fundamentals of purchasing fresh produce in the wholesale markets on Dock Street in Philadelphia. I soon knew that this is what I enjoyed doing.

We added retail markets and expanded the amount and varieties of fruits and produce we grew. Still we knew that in order to make our retail markets a more complete place for our customers to shop we would need to have available much more to sell. This gave me the opportunity to sharpen my buying skills. At the Food Center in Philadelphia I was known to hackle to get even a nickel a box off the asking price of a wholesale fruit or produce item. Early on I would travel with my straight job truck, sometimes as far as Eaton, North Carolina for cantaloupes and watermelon. I purchased many loads of watermelons and cantaloupes over the years at the Farmer's Auction in North Carolina and later in the season at Laurel, Delaware. We would extend the season for our customers beyond what was available and shipped form California. My goal was to always buy the best quality and the sweetest at the best value. The watermelons were unloaded at our markets. At the Lehigh

Street, Emmaus market we had space to unload a full trailer, stacking them right on the floor. At the Union Boulevard market in Allentown and the Easton Avenue market in Bethlehem our space was more limited and we could only unload a half a trailer load at each of those markets.

Buying produce can be a very tricky business. You need to know the supply and demand. Prices are based on that. You make the deal. You stick with the price. It is not always as profitable as you had hoped.

As I reminisce and think about those years of buying and selling produce I remember a particular Memorial Day Weekend. I made sure that I was at the Food Center in Philadelphia late on Friday morning. This is when there were often special deals to be made. The merchants were trying to sell everything they had by the end of the day. Strawberries arrived by tractor trailer from California too late to make the busy part of the sales day. I was offered the full load, forty-two pallets. Each pallet had ninety-six flats. The total 4,062 flats each had twelve pints on them. We sold all 48,744 pints that weekend in our three retail markets and our stands at Allentown Fairgrounds Market and Zern's Market in Gilbertsville. It was a busy weekend for all of us.

I recall a season when Bing cherries were very scarce. Again on a Friday morning a load came to the Food Center, a late arrival from California. The merchant contacted me to see if I could use them. I bought them all and we sold them all that weekend. They were the only Bing cherries available in our area.

During our busiest season it took a lot of produce to supply our own three markets and the two market stands; up to two hundred tons of produce per week which would fill ten tractor trailer loads. The produce came from both our own fields and wholesale purchases. It takes a lot of my time to purchase what we needed. I would go to Philadelphia Produce Center early on Tuesday morning to do my buying, and then fly to Columbia, South Carolina to buy at their terminal farmer's market. This would start in late June when their tomatoes, melons, peaches and more were ready for retail markets weeks before our local crops were ready to harvest. Then I would fly back to Philadelphia on Wednesday evening, do more buying there on early Thursday morning and return home. There were times when I also made a trip to John's Island, South Carolina to purchase tomatoes.

A lot of hard work and hand work went into providing sweet corn for our markets. We grew white, yellow and bi-color corn and tried to have each variety available at each of our markets. We invested in a sweet corn picker which took off all the ears in one row at a time. The ears were elevated into by conveyor belt into a wagon that was towed behind the picker. This eliminated a lot of hand work and got the fresh picked corn to the packing house quicker. We now could also start picking corn at 3 AM. The fresh picked ears arrived at the packing house as early as 7 AM. In the packing house the ears were graded and packed for shipping to our markets. They arrived at the markets by 9 AM during the peak of the sweet corn season. It was always important to us to get sweet corn to the markets fresh. Our markets were always stocked with fresh sweet corn for the Fourth of July holiday weekend. Our own was not ready that early in the season. We would purchase it from a grower in Delaware. Our truck would continue to pick up a load early each morning until our crop was ready.

Though wearing, I kept this schedule for a number of years. In 1987, after a diagnosis of heart problems, it was time to start thinking of how to solve this concern. We decided it was time to sell all the markets and stop growing edible produce. Our time and energies would now be focused on the wholesale greenhouse business. The day of the store equipment auction sale was one of my hardest days.

We have learned a lot about greenhouse growing over the years. When I think back to the time we first started growing in the greenhouse, how hard and inconvenient most everything was. We had small greenhouses, with narrow aisles. Everything had to be carried in and out. We had our trucks fitted out with shelves using 2"X12" boards, 5 or 6 levels. This was a lot of slow heavy work to get the trucks loaded and unloaded.

When we first started growing Easter flowers we had no refrigerated bulb storage. This is a necessary step so that growing of a bulb can be started and the plant growth held before it is forced into bloom. We *would bury the bulbs into a cold frame area outside and cover them with sawdust. Sometimes it worked out okay, but more often than not especially if Easter was early, everything would be frozen together. If Easter was late, in the warmth of early spring the bulbs would force up out of the cover. It was far from ideal. Today in our greenhouses everything is loaded onto rolling carts or packed into boxes that can be lifted by forklifts. Bulbs are now stored in refrigerated bulb rooms which makes it easy to take any out and place them in the greenhouse growing areas. Ready when we need them to be. It continues to be an operation involving many man hours of labor, but not as hard physically as in our early years.*

In 2003 and 2004 when the development of homes was going at a fast pace we were offered what seemed to be a good investment in what we thought was a solid company. We had previous successful investments with this group, a development in Central Bucks and one in New Jersey. We were satisfied with the offered good rate of interest on our proposed investment in what we believed was a good opportunity. We invested heavily on the purchase of two local farms that were next to each other. This land was to be developed into multiple subdivisions for single homes. Everything appeared to be going well. We kept investing more. At 30% interest, what could be better? The project moved slowly due to all the red tape and township demands for approvals. And then the housing market crashed. We were left holding on to nothing. It was a very expensive lesson; we lost our entire two and a half million dollar investment. But thanks be to God. We still had our health and could keep pressing onward.

We will always be thankful the many wonderful employees that we had through all the years. For several, it was the only job they ever held. Others tried other jobs, but returned after a short time away. Eight of our longtime employees are now, as of August 1, 2012, the owners of our company. I remain employed with Dan Schantz Farm and Greenhouses, LLC as a consultant and in charge of the Lehigh Street store. I still am involved with our other investments. We have a number of current sites and some in the making.

Many deals were made over the years. Mildred was always supportive and trusted our decisions, even when it turned out not to have been the best choice.

I always say that I am a produce man at heart. Even today that is what I think about and what most of my dreams are about; buying and selling produce. The greenhouse business has been very rewarding; the beauty of a finished crop ready to be shipped always brings much satisfaction. I remember many joys and some sorrows. It has been an interesting and sometimes challenging journey. I tried and I enjoyed success. I have also failed in some endeavors. I have many good memories and some I wish I could forget. I am thankful to God for good health, a loving wife and a great family. I am grateful for the opportunities that came to us. I am thankful for the many good employees that have worked for us for many years.

Mildred's Reminiscing

" *T*hinking back over the last sixty years brings back all kinds of memories and emotions.

We were young when we married on a hot August day. We were both eager to start our lifetime together.

We started with very little. Our first home together was a one bedroom apartment on the third floor of a renovated barn in the neighborhood where we grew up. We lived there for three and a half years until we purchased our farm in Lower Milford Township where we lived for thirty-seven years.

We both wanted children. After eight years of marriage we were blessed with our first child through the adoption of a two and a half day old baby boy. We named him Thomas Lee. He grew to be a healthy active little boy. Two years later we received through adoption, our three and a half day old little baby girl. We named her Connie Lynn. Now we had our ideal, complete family.

Time never stands still and as our family grew so did our business. Both our family and the business demanded more of my time. I knew I could not do justice to both. I needed help around the house. I had several helpers but it was Betty Urffer, a neighboring teenager, who was very helpful and dependable. She would later marry Bob Hummel. She helped us for many years, all through her growing up, her marriage and after she had her own children. I have always said that I don't mind working hard, but I can't handle coming back to a messy home. Betty always had things in order for which I was grateful.

During the years that we grew many varieties of fruit and vegetables I would spend a lot of my time in the packing house. This is where we would wash, sort, pack and refrigerate everything for our retail markets or wholesale buyers. Fridays and Saturdays were busy market days for me. Our produce stand at the Allentown Fairgrounds Market was a busy place. Sales would start early Friday morning so everything had to be set up on Thursday. Sallie Urffer a long time employee who started working for us as a teenager could handle most any assigned job. She was really talented at displaying produce in an attractive way.

Dan would give her a diagram or talk to her about the special items to be featured and how much space should be given to each variety. She would then make sure each item had the right amount of space and that the colors would blend attractively. Sallie had a big heart and everyone enjoyed working with her. I would help at our Allentown Fairgrounds Markets stand in the morning on Fridays and then go to the Gilbertsville Market to get things set up and ready for selling. In the years after the markets were sold I spent more time in the greenhouses. When we first started greenhouse growing, we both had lots to learn. It is quite different from field growing. But we learned as we grew and kept adding new greenhouses.

In the early 1960's we enclosed the back porch and made this our business office. I did all the office work; payroll and bookkeeping for a number of years until it became too much to do for me. We then hired part time help for a number of years. In 1969 we hired Joyce Heilman as our first full time office secretary and bookkeeper. Now my main duties were to care for our family, working at market two days a week and spending time in the packing house and the greenhouses. In 1973 a new office building was completed. The building has been expanded and is still used today as the business office. The office at the farmhouse was renovated into my all new laundry.

In the fall I would always help with the washing, shellacking and packing the gourds. This is when I would carefully select the best size, shape and color of the gourd crop for their seeds to be used for next year's crop. Since we now have equipment to wash, dry, wax and dry again I no longer select these for seeds myself. A long time employee does a good job in selecting the right ones. After the fall harvest season is over these selected gourds are broken open and the seeds removed. The seeds are spread out on trays and dried in the greenhouse for several weeks. They are then taken to a service where they are treated and inoculated to ensure that they are disease free. Some are sold to a seed company and listed in their catalog.

In my last number of years my job in the greenhouse was to go through every area of all the greenhouses. By now we had forty-two greenhouses plus all the gutter connected greenhouses to make a total of twenty-three acres of indoor growing areas plus as soon as spring temperatures allowed, hardy crops were grown outdoors on about twenty-three acres. I carefully looked over every crop and took notes and would make suggestions for the growers. To cover all these areas with my eyes it took most of two days each week. As I walked I took notes about each crop in each area. These notes were then given to Steve Thomas, our Supervisor of Greenhouse Operations. Steve would go over the notes with each of the growers who were in charge of a particular area and crop.

This was always an enjoyable time for me. To see the crops, start to finish; the beauty of a greenhouse full of flowering plants is hard to beat. This was also a way for me to see our employees and stay visible as an owner. Even today, when I make an appearance in the greenhouse, the growers ask when will I be coming back to make notes for them.

I did this until the time in 2012 when I started with a period of major illness. On a hot August evening in 2012, I went out to water our plants outside our home. Since I had had a number of knee replacements, I wasn't as steady on my feet as I used to be. I fell and landed on the hot macadam right next to the end of our pavement. I couldn't get up and Dan did not hear me call to him. I sat out on that hot macadam for about twenty minutes until he did hear me. He helped me get up. I was overheated and upset but did not seem hurt. After about an hour I still didn't feel right so we decided to go to the emergency room at Grand View Hospital in Sellersville. There they determined that I had a mild heart attack. They sent me to Lehigh Valley Hospital in Allentown for further testing. After a heart catheterization was done I was told I needed open heart surgery. A triple heart bypass surgery was done the next day. All went well. I was discharged and doing okay at home until I suddenly had severe pain in my left knee. We took a trip back to the emergency room where it was determined that I had a serious knee infection. I was admitted to the hospital and had surgery to try to clean out the infection. I was told that the knee prosthesis should have been removed for best results but because I had two previous knee replacement on that knee there was no longer enough remaining bone to remove the prosthesis and later replace it. The infection was cleaned out and packed with antibiotic crystals. I was also taking oral antibiotics in hopes that the infection would heal. For a time it appeared to be healing but in less than three weeks' time the wound was again very painful. Another surgery was performed on the knee. The wound would not heal. I went to wound care specialists. Nothing helped. On December 19, 2012 a third surgery was performed on the knee. It still did not heal.

For several months I had a wound V.A.C. devise strapped around my waist hoping to draw out the bad matter from the open wound. And about the same time my cardiologist determined I needed to wear a LifeVest defibrillator. So now I had two devises strapped around my body.

The orthopedic doctor told us that the wound would never heal. He suggested that the next surgery would be to remove my leg above the knee. I was not ready for that and decided to consult another doctor. At my appointment with a Doctor from the Rothman Group of Orthopedics I learned that there might be a 20 to 25% chance of saving my leg by removing the prosthesis and placing a rod in my left leg. The rod would be from just above the ankle to above the knee area. This surgery was done on March 1, 2013 at Jefferson Hospital in Philadelphia. During this surgery the surgeons also did a muscle flap. Taking muscle form the back of my calf and bringing it over the open wound. It was during this procedure that a nerve was damaged which has caused me to have a dropped foot. I was taken directly to Manor Care Nursing in Bethlehem when I was discharged from Jefferson Hospital. I spent four weeks in that facility before returning home. I still had a lot of adjusting to do with my now permanently straight leg.

During my recovery from this surgery it was now time to have my pacemaker upgraded and also to have a defibrillator devise. Another surgery.

By July of 2013 all my knee and leg wounds were healed. I was feeling pretty good. But at some point in August I noticed a sore spot on my left big toe. The podiatrist sent me to a wound care specialist. It just kept getting worse. Nothing helped.

After many doctor visits and consultations I was told that I did not have enough blood flowing down to my foot. Doctors had varied opinions. One thought part of my toe should be amputated. Another thought the entire big toe had to be removed before it would heal. I had two unsuccessful catheterization procedures in an attempt to open the veins in my leg. Finally I was now told by another doctor that by-pass surgery might be the answer. This seemed to be the option with the most promise. On December 5, 2013 I had surgery. I now have good blood flow to my foot. The wound started to look better. And finally by the middle of February, 2014 I had my last doctor visit. My toe is completely healed. It is a bit misshapen but that is okay. I still have two legs and ten toes.

Through this reminiscing I don't want to leave the impression that these sixty plus years were always without problems or concerns. We had bad days—days where everything seemed to go wrong. With faith and trust I have tried not to worry. I have strived to keep my head up and keep pressing forward.

I'm thankful for the many blessings God has given us and for Dan, my loving husband, friend and partner. We have had a great journey these last sixty plus years with our great family, children, grandchildren and great grandchildren. What a joy it has been to watch them quickly grow and mature and become the very special people they are. There have been trials along the way but the happy memories far outweigh any others. Our children, grandchildren and great grandchildren live in a computer world that I will never understand. But I wish them all God's blessings and pray that they will all keep their eyes and their hearts in His will.

God has been good to us and we are thankful for each day.

Employees

Many long time employees are shared as part of the stories of the business ventures and personal lives of Dan and Mildred. All could not possibly be included. All are near and dear to Dan and Mildred. Whenever a valued employee decided he or she needed a change in employment Dan would always encourage them and tell them if it didn't work out, they would be welcomed back.

Mildred shares her thoughts and memories of many of the longtime employees:

Joyce Heilman was hired in 1968 as Dan's first secretary. She faithfully continued in this role until 1994. In addition, from 1970 until 2013 she assumed on the role of Show Manager. She had complete control of the Antique & Memorabilia Shows held in several locations and held several times a year. The bi-annual Garage Sale held at the Agri-Plex of Allentown Fairgrounds was also under her management.

Joyce is and always will be more than an employee. She was the nice lady who did her work in the first office, a place that was connected to our kitchen at the farm house. Our children were very young when she started working for us so she sometimes found herself to be the babysitter for short periods of time. We always got along as friends. Joyce and Mildred still stay in close touch by telephone and sometimes for lunch. She has a strong Christian witness and enjoys her church and many friends and family.

Staring from the beginning, but not necessarily in order, we fondly remember these employees and their part in our journey.

Virginia "Ginny" Bauder was a young neighbor girl who was the first seasonal full-time employee. She worked at the first road stand on Route 309 in Quakertown. She later became its manager and there for several years. She now lives out of the area and operates her own farm and orchard and has a road stand operation.

Pauline Fritz worked for many years at the Spinnerstown farm greenhouses until she retired. She was very dependable, pleasant and continually eager to do a good job; we will always miss her.

Sue Barberry came to work for us at the retail greenhouse of the Big Barn store. She is very talented and a 'people' person. She soon became the manager of the store's greenhouse. She took time off to raise her family and is now working for us again as the Assistant Manager of the Dan Schantz Greenhouse and Cut Flower Outlet in Allentown.

Angie Toth was the retail greenhouse manager at the Lehigh Street store in Allentown and later at the Dan Schantz Greenhouse and Cut Flower Outlet in Bethlehem. A very talented and energetic lady was a valuable employee. We lost her in 2011 when she lost her battle with cancer.

Dick and Mavis Swartley served together in the late seventies. Dick, as the farm operations manager, worked in the fields and with the migrant men. Mavis, could be found in the greenhouses where she worked the automatic seeder as one of her responsibilities. When each of their children was old enough they worked at the farm or helped out at the farm market stands. They served well for over 15 years.

Dick and a migrant worker had a serious falling out at one time. I don't recall what the problem was but this man was out to get Dick. During this time of the season when you usually could be find Dick out picking sweet corn early in the morning on the machine picker. This man was waiting for Dick with a gun. He shot who he thought was Dick on the machinery, but that morning it was not. Instead he shot and wounded Arthur Weaver in the arm. Arthur did recover. The shooter was found guilty and did serve prison time.

Evelyn "Evie" Sadrovitz did everything necessary to run a smooth operation in the "check out" area and served in the customer service booth at the Big Barn Market on Lehigh Street.

Chris Heilman worked in general duties when she first started. Later she was promoted to general greenhouse manager at the greenhouse built on the property of Big Barn Farm Market. This was after the Big Barn Market had been sold in 1987 to a car dealership. She was the store and greenhouse manager at the Dan Schantz Greenhouse and Cut Flower outlet in Bethlehem.

Ray Smith *worked as a farmer and farm equipment operator. He did much of the tractor and field work while we were still growing vegetables. Now he is still active in doing whatever needs to be done. He spends most of his time driving truck delivering or picking up plants from either of our growing locations.*

Juan Rivera *has been faithfully serving our company since 1978. He and his wife, Carmen, who also worked in the greenhouse for many years, are living in Allentown. He also drives truck delivering or picking up plants to either of our locations.*

Cindy Thomas *is one of the most artistic people I know. She originally started as pumpkin painter, mainly for retail. Her job moved into the responsibilities of getting things together, researching paints and designs for the pumpkin and gourd painters. Today she draws all the patterns for each size we paint. She also does the newspaper advertisements, using her talents to create our attractive color ads. She is married to Steve Thomas, who is a partner in Dan Schantz Farm and* **Greenhouses, LLC.**

Sharon Hyndman *has worked in the sales department since 1992. She is also very talented in making up brochures and advertising materials. She is the one who talks to our sales representative in China, placing orders for the various items we add on to the painted pumpkins and character mums. She is in charge of all of the fundraisers that we offer to churches, schools, clubs, etc. The fundraisers are more common in the spring when annuals and hanging baskets are sold. She is also in charge of the orders from churches. We now have close to one hundred churches purchasing their Christmas Poinsettias and also their Easter lilies.*

Larry Geissinger, *my nephew, has done many and varied things in his life. He has worked for us in between other jobs and after several years in voluntary service. He and his wife, Libby own the Quakertown farm which was the last home of my parents, Clarence and Maggie Geissinger. We built a three and a half acre greenhouse on a portion of this farm and are in a lease agreement with Larry.*

Kevin Hench came to us from Chambersville, Pennsylvania in 1978. He was recently married and just 21 years old. He and his wife lived in the apartment of the converted labor camp building on the farm property. Kevin left in 1990 and returned in 2002, and has been here since that time. Kevin works as the assistant to Patrick Flanley. He is in greenhouse production and shipping; always making sure that the right UPC stickers are on everything; that everything is done on time and that as he often has heard Dan say, he wants "wheels under them trucks."

Mark Ringenary is a great guy who worked here for a number of years, then decided he needed a change. After a few years, he is back with us again. He is at our main farm location in greenhouse production and shipping. He is another one who does whatever needs to be done to keep everything running efficiently including the transplanters and the line. These run smoothly and work properly under Mark's watchful eye.

Kevin Echevarria is the grower and general manager at our Pipersville location. He worked at our main farm location for a number of years. He then took employment with the prior owners of the Pipersville greenhouses. After we purchased the location, he stayed on and is doing a good job.

Nigel Smith is the manager of the Rising Sun greenhouse in Rising Sun, Maryland. Hardworking Nigel expertly runs the day to day operations of the greenhouse and utilizes the greenhouse space for maximum yield. Nigel is a people person, respected by those who work with him. Originally from southern England, Nigel is considered an innovator who is known throughout the horticultural industry.

Brenda Szukics is the retail manager of our Allentown store. She started working for us as a checker. It was clear that she should become an Assistant Manager of the store and was then promoted to Manager. Brenda sees what needs to be done and does it or makes sure it is done and done correctly. One rule in the retail greenhouse she is sure to stick by is to never put that white mums next to the yellow ones. Dan prefers it that way. She makes sure it is done. She is a dedicated, knowledgeable employee with lots of energy. Brenda always enjoyed our company picnics and dinners.

Mildred's Recipes ~ Everyone's favorites

T here isn't a friend or employee that does not extol Dan and Mildred's gift of hospitality. They graciously host gatherings for friends, family employees and church groups. Mildred is famous for her strawberry dessert and many other well-loved dishes. Their story would not be complete without including a few favorites and those most requested.

Mildred's Strawberry Dessert

This recipe is a favorite with the employees Dan Schantz Farm as well as their family and friends. Mildred suggests also trying it with fresh peaches and peach glaze. Raspberries and other fruit work well with purchased or homemade glaze. Cut the recipe in half to make a 9-10" pie.

Ingredients:

2 Qts or 3 lbs	Fresh strawberries, reserve 6.
1 – 8 oz.	Cream Cheese, softened.
1 – 12 oz.	Cool Whip
2 – T.	Sugar
2 - 13.5 oz	Strawberry Glaze
1 – 8 oz.	Cool Whip
2 cups	Graham Cracker crumbs
½ cup	Butter, softened
¼ cup	Sugar

Directions:

Reserve and wash six of the nicest whole strawberries with stem and leaves for the garnish.

Strawberry Filling. Wash and cut up strawberries. Mix well with the glaze until all berries are coated. Use all the glaze or as much as you like depending on how sweet and gooey you like it. Set aside.

Prepare Crust. Mix ingredients well and press into the bottom and up sides of a 9X13" dish. Set aside.

Cream Cheese filling. Mix cream cheese, sugar and the 12 oz. container of Cool Whip. Beat until smooth. Set aside.

Assemble. Gently spoon Cream Cheese filling onto Graham Crust. Smooth evenly. Top with strawberry mixture. Refrigerate. Just before serving, spread 8 oz. container of Cool Whip on top of strawberry filling. Cut the 6 strawberries reserved for garnish in half leaving on the greens and arrange on top.

Apple Torte

Ingredients:

½ cup + 2 T.	Butter, divided
1 ½ cups	Sugar, divided. You will use in 3 parts
1 ¼ cups +2T	Flour, divided
8 oz.	Cream cheese
1 large	Egg
1 ½ tsp.	Vanilla, divided
6 cups	Baking apples, cored, peeled and sliced
1 tsp.	Cinnamon
½ cup	Sliced almonds
6 cups	Apples Peeled, cored and cut into pieces. Mildred prefers using Macintosh or Cortland Apples

Directions:

Assemble Crust: Mix ½ cup butter, ½ cup sugar, 1 ¼ cups flour and ½ tsp. vanilla. Press into a 10" spring form pan. Bake at 450 degrees for 6 minutes. Set aside.

Bottom layer: Mix Cream cheese, egg, ¼ cup sugar and 1 tsp. vanilla. Beat until smooth. Pour over sweet crust and set aside.

Top layer: Mix cinnamon,¾ cup sugar and 2 Tablespoons flour. Toss with apples and almonds until all are well-coated. Put apple/almond mixture on top of cream cheese mixture. Dot with 2 tablespoons butter and sprinkle with 2 Tablespoons of water.

Bake in preheated oven at 450 degrees for 10 minutes.

Reduce heat to 400 degrees and bake an additional 45 minutes. When cooled remove spring form and serve.

Applesauce

This recipe is for one batch. Mildred's daughter (Connie) and granddaughter (Chelsie) help each year and several batches are made at once. Mildred only uses yellow transparent apples for her applesauce.

Ingredients:

1 Bushel	Yellow Transparent Apples
	White sugar or Splenda to taste.
10-12 ounces	Water. Add or reduce water to achieve desired consistency.

Directions:

1. Wash and remove ends of each apples. Cut into quarters. Do not peel.

2. Place apples with water in a large 'boiler" pot. Cover.

3. Cook on medium/high until soft. About ten minutes. Stir often being sure to reach the bottom of the pot. Do not allow apples to brown or "catch" on sides or bottom of pot.

4. Run cooked apples through a sieve (Mildred uses a Victoria Strainer) into a large container.

5. Stir in sugar or sugar substitute.

6. Allow to cool. Package for freezing or canning according general food industry recommendations.

Mildred's Cutout Cookies　　　　**Makes about 6 dozen cookies**

*Mildred's recipe is adapted from the Mennonite Community Cookbook.
Her granddaughter (Niki) helped make a double batch each Christmas.
They are cookies that are flavored with love more that ingredients.*

Ingredients:

1 cup	Shortening (Use half butter for good flavor)
2 cups	Sugar (granulated)
2	Eggs
5 cups	Flour (approximately)
1 tsp.	Salt
1 tsp.	Baking Soda
¼ cup	Milk
1 tsp.	Vanilla

Directions:

- Cream shortening and sugar. Add vanilla.

- Add eggs and beat until fluffy.

- Sift flour. Measure and stir in salt and soda.

- Add sifted dry ingredients to batter, alternating with milk.

- Stir until dough is smooth.

- Chill for several hours.

- Roll out to ¼ inch thick. Cut fancy shapes.

- Place one inch apart on a greased cookie sheet. Sprinkle as desired with colored sugar.

- Bake at 400 degrees for 8 to 10 minutes.

Oyster Filling

This recipe is a Schantz family favorite Thanksgiving side dish.

Ingredients:

8 dozen	Stewing Oysters
20 oz.	Oyster Crackers (2 - 10 ounce boxes)
1 cup	Butter (2 sticks)
1 tsp.	Pepper
1 T.	Salt
1 pint	Whole milk

Directions:

- Crush the crackers and place them in a large bowl.

- Drain the oysters. Reserve the juice. Cut oysters in half.

- Mix oysters with crushed crackers. Add one pint of reserved liquid and salt and pepper. Allow to set for one to one and half hours.

- Heat milk with the butter until the butter is just melted.

- Add milk/butter to the oyster cracker mixture. Mixture should be moist, slightly wet consistency. Add additional milk or oyster juice as needed to obtain consistency.

- Place filling in a baking dish and bake at 350 degrees for 1 hour 15 minutes. Stir frequently.

Stuffed Peppers

Dan loves eating the produce he is passionate about growing. This is a favorite dish of Dan's from Mildred's collection. She makes dozens and freezes them for easy meals later.

Ingredients:

6	Colored Fresh Peppers (This type is sweeter than green peppers.)
Filling	1 Pound Ground Beef
	1 small onion, chopped
	2 tsp. salt, divided
	1/2 cup rice (cook rice as directed on the package)
	Dash of pepper
1 quart	Tomato Juice Cocktail

Directions:

- Wash, core and remove all seeds from each of the peppers. Cut each pepper in half.

- Blanch peppers before stuffing to remove any bitterness. Boil water in large stockpot. Add one teaspoon salt to the water. Blanch peppers for 5 minutes. Remove from water and drain.

- Brown beef and chopped onion in a skillet. Add 1 teaspoon salt and dash of pepper. Stir in cooked rice. Set aside.

- Place cooled peppers in a casserole dish. Fill each with meat/rice mixture. Prepared peppers can be tightly covered and frozen at this point.

To cook: Cover freshly made or defrosted peppers with tomato juice cocktail. Bake at 350 degrees for 1½ hours.